To
The Most Sacred Heart of Jesus,
The Most Sorrowful and Immaculate Heart of Mary,
For the Honor of St. Raymond of Peñafort,
For my beloved wife Tatyana

The **Third Secret of Fatima** & The **Synodal Church**

Vol. I. *Pope Benedict's Resignation*

Edmund J. Mazza, PhD

"You know what withholdeth, that he [Antichrist] may be revealed in his time. For the mystery of iniquity already worketh; only that he who now holdeth, do hold, until he be taken out of the way. And then that wicked one shall be revealed"

2 Thessalonians 2: 6-7

"So whatever he [Pope Benedict] was doing, *he wasn't resigning the papacy. That's the mystery which will be explained by the [third] Secret... Our Lady* [of Fatima] *will explain it to you in those...25 lines that have not been revealed."*

Father Nicholas Gruner, Deerfield Address, 2014

"...that third part of the Secret of Fatima in which, in all likelihood, Our Lady foretold the apostasy of the Hierarchy with the Second Vatican Council and the liturgical reform."

Archbishop Carlo Maria Vigano, Homily for the Feast of the Chair of St. Peter in Rome, 2023

"[Tyconius] distinguishes a dark Church, composed of the *populus malus* of Satan, and a *decora*, honest Church, composed of Christ's faithful. In the present state, the two bodies of the Church are inseparably commingled, but according to the Apostle's prediction, *they will be divided at the end of days*: "Now this goes on from the time of the Lord's passion *until the church, which keeps it in check, withdraws* from the midst of this mystery of lawlessness [*mysterium facinoris*] so that godlessness may be unveiled in its own time"...an eschatological time...goes from Christ's passion up to the "mystery of lawlessness," when the separation of the bipartite body of the Church will be realized... [A]t the end of the fourth century there were authors who had identified the *Church itself as the katechon.*"

Giorgio Agamben, *The Mystery of Evil: Benedict XVI and the End of Days*, 2013

"It is not to be excluded that I will enter history as the one who split the Catholic Church."

Pope Francis/Jorge Bergoglio, 2016

"In the Holy Place itself, where has been set up the See of the most blessed Peter and the Chair of Truth for the light of the world, they have raised the throne of their abominable impiety, with the iniquitous design that when the Pastor has been struck, the sheep may be scattered."

Pope Leo XIII, From the St. Michael Exorcism Prayer, 1890

"Apropos of what is said in a certain Gloss, namely, that 'I withstood him as an adversary,' the answer is that the Apostle [Paul] opposed Peter in the exercise of authority, not in his authority of ruling. Therefore from the foregoing we have an example: prelates, indeed, an example of humility, that they not disdain corrections from those who are lower and subject to them; *subjects have an example of zeal and freedom, that they fear not to correct their prelates, particularly if their crime is public and verges upon danger to the multitude.*"

St. Thomas Aquinas, *Commentary on Galatians* 2: 11-13

Table of Contents

Acknowledgements

It goes without saying that any faults in this work are, of course, entirely my own. If anything I have written is not in accord with the authentic Magisterium of the Roman Catholic Church, I hereby recant it.

As any author, I owe a great debt of gratitude to a great many, but I wish to especially thank the following persons:

My deepest gratitude goes out to Sister Shanna Byrne, Liz Yore, Steve Mosher, Fred Martinez, "Mary's Secretary," Guido Ferro Canale, George Andrie, Pierre Azzi and others for reading drafts of the manuscript and/or offering most welcome revisions and comprehensive suggestions.

I am very grateful to Ann Barnhardt, Mark Docherty, and "Supernerd" (especially for trailblazing the path) and all the others without whose friendship, prayers, and practical assistance, this book would not have been possible.

Lastly, my deepest debt owed is to my dearest muse, Tatyana…

Because her simplicity, it seems,
Is ignorant of deceit, and still she
Believes completely in her dreams…

Because she's trusting, and honest
And by Heaven has been blessed,
With profound imagination,
A fiery will, a lively mind,
A soul for passion's fires designed,
A spirit tuned to all creation

January 23, 2023
Traditional Feast Day of
St. Raymond of Peñafort, OP
Editor of the Code of Canon Law (1234-1917)

Author's Preface
"...since Judas kissed Jesus"

"World enslavement or peace, it's up to the Pope."
Father Nicholas Gruner

"But as in the [Second Vatican] Council, even in the new Code [of Canon Law] *'munus'*...not infrequently also...[has] *a special, theological meaning* of the *three munera [gifts]* of Christ (can. 204 § 1) and of the Church...passages in which the legislator speaks of the "*munus*" of Peter (can. 331) or *the Roman Pontiff* (can. 332 § 2, 333 §§ 1-2, 334) *are connected with this sense.*"[1]
Cardinal Peter Erdö, 1989

"Then indeed the Roman clergy, stripping [Pope] Liberius of his pontifical dignity, went over to Felix, whom they knew [then] to be a Catholic. From that time, Felix began to be the true Pontiff. For *although Liberius was not a heretic, nevertheless he was considered one*, on account of the peace he made with the Arians, and *by that presumption the pontificate could rightly [merito] be taken from him: **for men are not bound, or able to read hearts; but when they see that someone is a heretic by his external works, they judge him to be a heretic pure and simple [simpliciter], and condemn him as a heretic.**"[2]
Cardinal St. Robert Bellarmine, *On the Roman Pontiff*, 1610

Follow the *Munus*

Since 1988 (when I was seventeen), my *"starets"* has been the world's foremost expert on the message of Our Lady of Fatima, the late, great Father Nicolas Gruner (1941-2015). In

---

[1] Peter Erdö, "*Ministerium, munus* et *officium* in codice Iuris canonici," *Periodica de re morali canonica liturgica*, vol. 78, no. 4 (1989), pp. 411-436; 428. All emphases in this book are mine, unless otherwise noted.

[2] http://strobertbellarmine.net/bellarm.htm

October 2014, in Deerfield, Illinois, Fr. Gruner quite startled his listeners when addressing Pope Benedict's resignation:

> So, there is this impression now created by the fact that Benedict when he resigned...before the resignation took effect, *if anything took effect* on February 27, 2012 [sic], he says, very clearly and you can read it for yourself, Benedict in his resignation says, **"I am not resigning the** *munus;"* M-U-N-U-S, that means in Latin, it's the office.

> Yet Canon Law...Canon 332...says, "if a pope were to resign, he must resign the *munus."* So here you have canon law saying, "to resign, you must resign the *munus."* And here you have Pope Benedict saying, "I'm not resigning the *munus."* Now to me, that's a...contradiction...*So whatever he was doing, he wasn't resigning the papacy. That's the mystery which will be explained by the [third] Secret...Our Lady will explain it to you in those...25 lines that have not been revealed."* [3]

According to Robert Ryan from Ireland:

> ...a month before Fr. Nicholas Gruner died, I collected him at the airport for a 2-hour drive to his Mass. I will never forget his words, "Robert, *Bergoglio is not the Pope, you*

[3] https://vimeo.com/228833627? embedded=true&source=vimeo_logo&owner=12213053; Benedict explicitly renounced only "the *ministerium* of the bishop of Rome," but when canon law speaks of the papacy, it uses the broader term *munus Petrinum.* As Cardinal Peter Erdö explains, *munus* is used in the sense of sacramental gift-commission from Christ: *"Sed sicut in Concilio, etiam in novo Codice «munus» intra limites huius secundi sensus principalis, haud raro etiam significatione speciali, theologica trium munerum Christi* (can. 204 § 1) *et Ecclesiae* (tac. 747; tac. 834) *apparet* (cf. can. 375 § 2, 519). *Cum hoc sensu connectuntur foci, in quibus legislator de «munere» Petri* (can. 331) *aut Romani Pontificis* (can. 332 § 2, 333 §§ 1-2, 334) *loquitur."* My translation from the Latin.

must read Benedict's resignation in Latin. Ratzinger is the Pope."[4]

As his associate in Our Lady's apostolate for more than 30 years, Father Paul Kramer, said of him:

As his unexpected death approached, Fr. Gruner became ever more convinced of the urgency to prove with a mass of evidence and sound argumentation *that Benedict XVI remains in office as the sole Vicar of Christ on earth; and that Francis is a manifest heretic* who cannot validly occupy the papal throne.[5]

Of such my own humble inquiries are made (for a profound debt owed).

Notes of caution: Although there is a body of evidence that Pope Benedict was "forced" to resign by his enemies, such is not the thesis of this work; nor that Benedict resigned so as to *willfully* deny the Office of Vicar of Christ to the next Bishop of Rome,[6] though, *in his own words,* "anything can be."[7]

"Why does this question make people irrationally angry?"

On January 27, 2023, Dr. Taylor Marshall released the results of his Twitter poll: "Is Pope Francis (today) the real, valid and true Pope of the Catholic Church?"[8] With more than 10,000

---

[4] YouTube comment February 15, 2022.

[5] Fr. Paul Kramer, *To Deceive the Elect,* (Sycamore, IL: Gondolin Press, 2019), Kindle Edition.

[6] Dr. Taylor Marshall interview, May 2020; https://www.youtube.com/watch?v=bABWi2CoVlc&t=2099s

[7] Peter Seewald, Benedict XVI, *Last Testament: In His Own Words,* (New York: Bloomsbury Continuum, 2016) Kindle Edition.

[8] https://twitter.com/TaylorRMarshall/status/1619011583933571073

total votes tabulated, only 46% said, "Yes." Marshall prefaced his tweet by asking: "Why does this question make people irrationally angry?"

Why, indeed?

In December of 2018, Ryan Grant authored an article at *One Peter Five*, entitled, "Rise of the Benevacantists," in which he compared Catholics who question the validity of Pope Benedict XVI's resignation and, therefore, the papacy of Pope Francis, to schismatics and Sedevacantists. As he puts it:

> To overthrow due process, the gift of the Church to the *legal systems* of the world, and reduce judgment of who the pope is to bloggers and Facebook posts opining from private judgment is to not only to attack the visibility of the Church, but to invite schism at levels unseen since the Middle Ages...

> Finally, if it is the case that Benedict is still pope and Francis is not, then this will be adjudicated by the Church, under the aegis of the current pontificate or a subsequent one. To formally declare, not to merely opine, feel, or secretly wonder, but to definitively declare Benedict's resignation invalid and Francis to not be the valid occupant, is nothing short of schismatic and to be avoided by all true Catholics.[9]

"This isn't a blockade"

As I read Grant's words they called to mind a dramatic scene from the silver screen.

---

[9] https://onepeterfive.com/benevacantists/

Thirteen Days (2000) is a film that recounts the harrowing story of those two weeks in late October 1962, known as "the Cuban Missile Crisis," a time when, if things had gone slightly differently, the planet would have experienced nuclear annihilation on such a scale, as to make Sodom and Gomorrah look like a KISS concert. (Then again, had WWIII happened, there would never have been "hard rock," or "glam rock," or a band named KISS, nor for that matter, would the Second Vatican Council have even finished its first session. Hmm…Well, who knew, there's a silver lining even to a mushroom cloud.)

The immanence of this Cold War apocalypse is brought home to the viewer in a tense exchange between Secretary of Defense Robert McNamara (played by veteran actor Dylan Baker) and an admiral by the name of Anderson. As those who are old enough to remember know (or who managed somehow to receive a competent American History education), JFK, upon learning of the presence in Cuba of nuclear weapons capable of hitting America, ordered a "quarantine" of that Communist country, one that would not allow Russian ships (carrying nukes) to reach the island. In the film, when the Russians fail either to turn back or reply to repeated hails, US warships suddenly *start firing*. The movie cuts to the command center where Secretary McNamara franticly orders the admiral to stand down. The visibly irritated admiral bleats out that they're only firing "starshells," that is, flares:

MCNAMARA
Starshells[?]

ADMIRAL ANDERSON
Get out of our way, Mr. Secretary. The
navy has been running blockades since
the days of John Paul Jones.

McNamara turns back. And all trepidation, embarrassment, hesitation are gone. He coldly appraises Anderson.

MCNAMARA

I believe the President made it clear
that there would be no firing on ships
without his express permission.

ADMIRAL ANDERSON

With all due respect, Mr. Secretary, we
were not firing on the ship. Firing on
a ship means attacking the ship. We
were not attacking the ship. We were
firing over it.

MCNAMARA

This was not the President's intention
when he gave that order. What if the
Soviets don't see the distinction? What
if they make the same mistake I just
did?   (beat)
There will be no firing anything near
ANY Soviet ships without my express
permission, is that understood, Admiral?

ADMIRAL ANDERSON

Yes, sir.

MCNAMARA

And I will only issue such instructions
when ordered to by the President.
        (beat)
John Paul Jones... you don't understand
a thing, do you, Admiral?

He passes his hand over the enormous plot below.

MCNAMARA (CONT'D)

This isn't a blockade.

McNamara, trembling with anger, awe, whirls to Anderson. And his burgeoning insight is born - clear, hard and cold.

MCNAMARA (CONT'D)

This, all this, is language, a new
vocabulary the likes of which the world
has never seen.
This is President Kennedy communicating
with Secretary Khruschev.[10]

Now, I am confident that Admiral Anderson was a patriot, a man totally dedicated to his country, just as I am likewise sure that Mr. Grant is a faithful Catholic who would do anything for the defense of Holy Mother Church, anything licit, at any rate. Yet, like the esteemed admiral, Grant (and scores of others) cannot seem to see the forest for the trees—*everything* is on the line and the difference between triumph and tragedy for millions of souls depends on whether those of us in the resistance comprehend the "new vocabulary," or like Mr. Grant, add more useless epithets like "Benevacantist" to an already overpopulated Catholic circular firing-squad.

I will limit my remarks to only one of the many facets of the resignation controversy raised in Grant's article, namely, the issue of Canon 188, which governs the resignation of Catholic prelates:

---

[10] https://www.dailyscript.com/scripts/13_days.html

A resignation made out of grave fear that is inflicted unjustly or out of malice, *substantial error,* or simony *is invalid by the law itself.*[11]

Archbishop Georg Gänswein

Among the authors whom Grant attacks are those who argue (based on the above canon) that Pope Benedict's resignation was invalid due to "substantial error." The substantial error alleged is that Pope Benedict XVI only resigned the *active* ministry of the papacy and not the contemplative. That is to say, the pontiff developed a new ontological understanding of the Petrine office— *one which still included him!* Repeatedly expressed by His Holiness —and his shadow, former Prefect of the Papal Household, Archbishop Georg Gänswein—this theological novelty was not even thinly disguised. As Gänswein told his audience on May 20, 2016, at the Pontifical Gregorian University in Rome:

This is why Benedict XVI has not given up either his name, or the white cassock. This is why the correct name by which to address him even today is "Your Holiness"; and this is also why he has not retired to a secluded monastery, but within the Vatican — as if he had only taken a step to the side to make room for his successor and a new stage in the history of the papacy...

But today we live with two living successors of Peter among us — who are not in a competitive relationship between themselves, and yet both have an extraordinary presence! ...Many people even today continue to see this new situation as a kind of exceptional (not regular) state of

---

[11] http://www.vatican.va/archive/ENG1104/_PN.HTM

the divinely instituted office of Peter (*eine Art göttlichen Ausnahmezustandes*)...

He has left the papal throne and yet, with the step made on February 11, 2013, he has not at all abandoned this ministry. Instead, he has complemented the personal office *with a collegial and synodal dimension, as a quasi-shared ministry* (*als einen quasi gemeinsamen Dienst*)[12]

This is clearly a departure from Church teaching. In two thousand years of history, the Church has never before taught such a "synodal" doctrine concerning the papacy. One can search the Bible, the Church Fathers, and all the pages of Denzinger from now till the crack of doom—and not find one such erroneous assertion. Yet, Grant criticizes those Catholics who see this as "grave error," as he writes:

To make the point even more obvious, Benedict himself has affirmed repeatedly that he did in fact resign, and he even defended his abdication to Cardinal Brandmüller, who had questioned its prudence. But then, some will say, what about Monsignor Gänswein, the pope's personal secretary, who said, "We have two popes"? This is often used by the Benevacantists as a smoking gun. Again, whatever a third party said, this would have to be determined in the external forum in an ecclesiastical court.

There are several points to be sorted out here:

---

[12] https://www.barnhardt.biz/2018/12/10/if-pope-benedict-is-the-first-ever-pope-emeritus-doesnt-that-mean-that-his-ontological-state-is-different-from-the-popes-who-actually-resigned/

Firstly, even if we stipulate that Benedict has affirmed repeatedly that he did in fact "resign," these affirmations are *not incompatible* with Gänswein's explanation of that resignation (nor for that matter are Gänswein's explanations about his explanation!)

Secondly, Grant considers Gänswein's testimony to be that of a "third party." Again, a legal technicality. Excuse me, the man had an official position as *Prefect of the Papal Household*. Are we expected to believe he's not a legitimate spokesman (with firsthand knowledge) for things "Papal"? He's the *one and only* man in the world who had intimate access on a daily basis with both Benedict and Bergoglio!

Furthermore, it is also clear to any reasonable person that Pope Benedict likely shares Gänswein's novel views, since—and this is critical—His Holiness NEVER came out publicly and DENOUNCED Gänswein. As Grant is fond of taking other Latinists to task: *Qui tacet consentit.*[13]

Lastly, Grant argues that third party testimony would have to be determined in the external forum by a Church court. This goes to the heart of his beef with the bloggers (I suspect with one in particular who knows a thing or two about animal husbandry): that they have taken it upon *themselves* to declare Benedict's resignation invalid. As he explains by way of analogy:

> To summarize the questions viz. Pope Benedict's completed and confirmed abdication, we can draw this sort of analogy. The consequence of individual laity "definitively declaring" Benedict's resignation to be invalid, on their own authority, is not at all different from a man who discovers that his marriage is invalid due to some

---

13 "Silence means approval."

impediment. Even if he were one hundred percent correct and this impediment were as plain as the summer sun, he cannot just run off and marry some other woman unless the Church has granted him a declaration of nullity, which is a judgment in the external forum. In other words, because the sacrament of matrimony is a public act, not unlike taking the office of the papacy or renouncing it, any defects affecting validity must be publicly adjudicated by the Church through the annulment process so that a definitive judgment will be issued and those concerned will have moral certitude on the matter.

Legalism only Encourages the Lawless

Now I completely agree with Grant that under *virtually* all circumstances, "a man who discovers that his marriage is invalid due to some impediment. Even if he were one hundred percent correct and this impediment were as plain as the summer sun, cannot just run off and marry some other woman" without an annulment as per Church law. Yet, would it not also be true that if such a man who had never been properly married in the eyes of God, *also had an extraordinary circumstance,* some *moral obstacle* (as opposed to mere personal whim, or fear of inconvenience, etc.), a threat to life or liberty, which kept him from seeking an annulment through ordinary channels, might he not then still enter his new marriage validly, no matter how technically illicit?[14] (After all, the principle of "equity" is based on the concept that lawmakers cannot conceive of *all* possible cases.)

Say, for example, the man was a Polish dissident behind the Iron Curtain in 1962. Suppose he was afraid to proceed through normal ecclesiastical courts because the Polish Church was riddled with communist spy-priests and bureaucratic informants?

---

[14] And provided that scandal be avoided at all costs.

Must our man really wait indefinitely (until 1989 and Fall of the Berlin Wall) in order to attempt marriage? (Interestingly enough, some scenario like this is the only hypothetical circumstance I can think of in which Francis's infamous Section 8, Footnote 351 of *Amoris Laetitia* could conceivably be squared with traditional Church teaching on remarried Catholics without annulments receiving the Eucharist.)

And now we have reached the crux of the matter. Grant is right, of course, that a *definitive* declaration of Benedict's resignation will require a Church pronouncement (which may or may not occur before the Three Days of Darkness and/or the Four Horsemen of the Apocalypse). Furthermore, any Catholic writer who advances the argument that Benedict was still Pope (BIP), or at least allows for the possibility, must add the caveat that his or her writings are entirely subject to the judgement of the authentic Magisterium of the One Holy Catholic Apostolic Church and that he or she totally abjures anything contrary to its ultimate pronouncements.

Nevertheless, Catholics (according to their competence) have a **"moral duty"** to exclaim what they believe to be the truth about the crisis we are facing. (As Canon 212, section 3 points out.[15]) There is probable doubt galore that Benedict's resignation was valid. To make an allegation based on a preponderance of the evidence should not be off limits. I hope Grant would not really expect us to believe that St. Catherine of Siena, for example (as everyone knows, the best female blogger of the 14th century) was morally bound NOT to tell Pope Gregory XI to go back to Rome

---

[15] "According to the knowledge, competence, and prestige which they possess, they have the right and even at times *the duty to manifest to the sacred pastors their opinion on matters which pertain to the good of the Church and to make their opinion known to the rest of the Christian faithful,* without prejudice to the integrity of faith and morals, with reverence toward their pastors, and attentive to common advantage and the dignity of persons." Canon 212 §3; http://www.vatican.va/archive/ENG1104/_PU.HTM

and stop persisting in his new-creative-ontological-Avignon-Petrine ministry until "adjudicated by the Church, under the aegis of the current pontificate or a subsequent one"? Was Catherine of Siena a schismatic? No, she was a doctor of the Church—that means she shows us the way. Nor, for that matter, was St. Vincent Ferrer a schismatic, though he lobbied people in good faith to follow (a man later officially declared by the Church) an antipope during the Great Western Schism.

To sum up, this is not a routine blockade. This is not the time to blithely trust that adherence to time-honored protocol will settle everything. This is not an existentially normal time in Church history: Almighty God, Himself, hurled bolts of lightning at the Dome of St. Peter's on the day of Benedict's resignation, a 300 page dossier (apparently lost through a wormhole in the Vatican necropolis along with the body of Jimmy Hoffa and Epstein's flight lists) was published at Benedict's request weeks earlier revealing that the Bark of Peter has been hijacked by an organized crime syndicate (whose favorite color is lavender); Francis knowingly gave an apartment to a sodomite priest who later hosted a cocaine-fueled orgy there (at the Congregation for the Doctrine of the Faith!),[16] and Francis and his favorites[17] recently claimed (with a straight face when they're not laughing[18]) that migration and plastic straws in the ocean[19] are apparently more pressing problems than addressing decades of sexual predation upon seminarians. We are dealing with evil inside the Church on a level unseen since Judas kissed Jesus.

---

[16] https://www.lifesitenews.com/news/breaking-pope-knowingly-gave-vatican-apartment-to-gay-priest-later-caught-i

[17] https://www.catholicworldreport.com/2018/08/28/cardinal-cupich-the-pope-has-a-bigger-agenda/

[18] https://www.faithwire.com/2018/09/14/vatican-releases-tone-deaf-image-of-pope-francis-laughing-with-cardinals-at-sex-abuse-meeting/

[19] https://www.nbcnews.com/news/world/pope-francis-urges-action-endless-fields-plastic-world-s-oceans-n905711

These lawless men are quite happy to see us hamstrung by our natural Catholic devotedness to law and tradition. Grant's attitude aids and abets them. With all due respect to him and to canon law,[20] let us acknowledge Saint Joseph, chaste-protector of the Holy Virgin Mary and Holy Mother Church, "a *just man, unwilling to expose her to the law*, decided to divorce her *privately*" (Matt. 1:19). Nor should we forget that by our Baptism we live in Christ Who IS Priest, Prophet, and King and we would do well to call to mind His words to the rigorous:

> And it came to pass again, as the Lord walked through the corn fields on the sabbath, that his disciples began to go forward, and to pluck the ears of corn. And the Pharisees said to him: Behold, why do they on the sabbath day that which is not *lawful*? And he said to them: Have you never read what David did when he had need, and was hungry himself, and they that were with him? How he went into the house of God, under Abiathar the high priest, and did eat the loaves of proposition, which was *not lawful* to eat but for the priests, and gave to them who were with him? And he said to them: *The sabbath was made for man, and not man for the sabbath.* Therefore the *Son of man is Lord of the sabbath* also. (Mark 2:23-27)

While only the Magisterium can *definitively* declare Benedict's resignation invalid and Francis not the valid occupant at the helm of Peter's Bark, that doesn't mean forthright clergy and laity cannot call it as they see it; nor does it give their

---

[20]As Bishop Schneider once responded with the words that "the SSPX is 'surely not schismatic.' In the bishop's eyes, it is 'a very narrow, legalistic view of the reality of the Church' which would lead to such a conclusion. Such a view is '*putting the letter of the Canon Law above the importance, the primary importance of the fullness of the Catholic faith* and of the traditional liturgy.' Bishop Schneider also sees a need to further clarify the term 'schism,' which, together with other terms, are 'subordinated' to the '*greatest law of Canon Law, which is the salvation of souls.*'"; https://www.lifesitenews.com/blogs/bp-schneider-communion-in-the-hand-a-grievous-evil-that-must-be-stopped/

detractors the right to tar-and-feather fellow Catholics in the trenches as Benevacantists or schismatics. (And while we're stowing our dark and gooey substances, let's also not forget that false shepherds are already plotting to muzzle faithful Catholic bloggers by means of synodal legislation and canon law,[21] so let's not be so eager to grease the skids for them.)

John Paul Jones, Mr. Grant? I tell you: "If these keep silent, the very stones will cry out!" (Luke 19:40)

---

[21] http://liturgicalnotes.blogspot.com/2018/10/censorship-bergoglianity-is-at-work-on.html;

Introduction

"There is no need to create another church [sic], but to create a different church [sic]."
Pope Francis/Jorge Bergoglio, October 2021

"The pope is…not the instrument through which one could…call a different Church into existence…"
Joseph Ratzinger, August 2002

Two Lightning Strikes, Two Popes

"…It was icy cold and raining sheets. When the storm started, I thought that lightning might strike…so I decided it was worth seeing whether – if it DID strike – I could get the shot at exactly the right moment."[1] That's how French Press Agency photographer, Filippo Monteforte, described the surreal scene in St. Peter's Square on the eerie evening of February 11, 2013, when two tremendous bolts of lightning, one after the other, struck the dome of the iconic Basilica. As another reporter put it: "As the sky was lit up by the huge bolt, it led to speculation as to whether Benedict XVI's boss was less than happy…the apparent divine intervention came as the 85-year-old pontiff sent shockwaves through the Church on Monday after announcing his retirement, the first pope to do so in 700 years."[2]

Joseph Ratzinger's resignation then led, in turn, to a situation *entirely* unprecedented in the 2,000-year history of the Catholic Church. For virtually the next decade in the Vatican City State, *two* men wore the signature white papal cassock, *two* men bestowed apostolic blessings on the faithful, and *two* men were formally addressed as "His Holiness." One resided in seclusion

---

[1] Paul Cockerton, "Lightning bolt hit Vatican not once but TWICE hours after Pope's shock resignation," *Mirror* (February 12, 2013); https://www.mirror.co.uk/news/world-news/lightning-bolt-hit-vatican-not-1705156

[2] "Bolt from the Blue," *On Demand News*; https://www.youtube.com/watch?v=7y_Ct38rLd8

and self-imposed silence, in prayer and meditation at the Mater Ecclesiae Monastery in the Vatican Gardens. The other still resides in the Domus Sanctae Marthae, the Vatican hotel, which was built to house visiting cardinals. Curiously, the Papal Apartments located in the Apostolic Palace which have been the official residence of the Popes since the 17th century—remain uninhabited.

The unexpected renunciation of Benedict and his perplexing presence in the Vatican as Pope Emeritus still confounds the faithful as much as—in some sense, even more than—the globalism and heterodoxy of the putative Pope, Francis.

An Evil "Pope"?

Former papal nuncio to the United States of America, His Excellency Archbishop Carlo Maria Vigano has expressed it this way:

But if it is humanly incredible and painful to have to recognize that a Pope may be evil, this does not allow us to deny the evidence, nor does it require us to resign ourselves passively to the abuse of power that he exercises in the name of God yet against God. And if no one will want to assault the Sacred Palace in order to drive out the unworthy guest, legitimate and proportionate forms of real opposition can be exercised, including pressure to resign and abandon the office. It is precisely in order to defend the Papacy and the sacred Authority it receives from the High and Eternal Priest that it is necessary to admonish one who humiliates it, demolishes it, or abuses it. I would even dare to say, for the sake of completeness, that also *the apparently arbitrary **renunciation of the exercise** of the sacred authority of the Roman Pontiff represents a very grave vulnus* [wound] *to*

2

the Papacy, and for this we must consider Benedict XVI responsible more than Bergoglio.[3]

Vigano's remarks raise many hard questions: Why did Pope Benedict "flee" his post, leaving the flock to be fleeced by a "Progressive" pontiff? Is it true that Benedict renounced only the "exercise" of the Roman bishop, not the papacy itself? (Is that even metaphysically possible?) *Can* a pope "be evil"? Can a legitimate Vicar of Christ abuse his power "against God" in an attempt to "demolish" Christ's Church? And have any (or all) of these things ever been foretold?

More than thirty years ago, in his bestseller, *The Keys of This Blood* (1991), exorcist and former aide to Cardinal Bea, Fr. Malachi Martin wrote: "Pope John Paul II and his papal bureaucracy have been pushed or have retreated into such ineffectual isolation from the day-to-day governance of the Church Universal, that now *three dreadful outcomes are possible.* Any of them could—probably would—entail the final disintegration of this Roman Catholic institutional organization..."[4]

The first possible outcome Martin predicted would be the day when: "a sizable body of...clergy and laity, become convinced —rightly or wrongly—that the then **occupant of the apostolic throne of Peter is not, perhaps never was, a validly elected pope.**"

The second possible equally destructive scenario would play out if such a sizable consensus one day reached the view— rightly or wrongly—that "the then occupant of the apostolic

---

[3] Archbishop Carlo Maria Vigano, "Open Letter To Confused Priests: Obedience, Resistance, Francis and Vaccines," January 30, 2021; as cited https://www.qoa.life/blogs/news/open-letter-to-confused-priests-vigano-on-obedience/. All emphases in this book are mine, unless otherwise noted.

[4] Malachi Martin, *The Keys of This Blood*, (New York, NY: Touchstone/Simon & Schuster, 1991), p. 677.

throne of Peter was elected quite validly but *over time had become heretical,* and was actually collaborating, actively or passively, in the *piece-by-piece dismemberment of the sacred Petrine Office...For a pope who became a heretic would cease to be pope...*"[5]

A third option that would tear the Church apart according to Martin would be the election of "a papal candidate whose policy would be to dissolve the unity and change the structure of the Roman Catholic Church by simply *abandoning the exercise of the Petrine Office...*it would also entail a new relationship of all bishops, including the bishop of Rome, to each other [synodality]."[6]

Martin put it perhaps most pointedly in a 1992 interview:

Martin: [...] what I think is fatally necessary for every Catholic to know, and that is *the fate of the papacy and the coming stress and danger: that we shall be without the strength of the papacy.*

Jansen: Is it ever possible that the cardinals at a future conclave could elect a heretical pope?

Martin: [brief pause over the sensitive nature of the question] You know...they have elected men in the past who had heretical ideas. Two or three. They have never elected yet an apostate...an apostate. [...] An apostate has rebelled against the very fundamental of faith and rejected God and Christ. We have apostates now who are *papabili* [men who could be elected pope]. *Yes, we could have an apostate.*[7]

---

[5] Ibid., p. 679.

[6] Ibid., p. 681.

[7] "Kingdom of Darkness," Malachi Martin Interview with Bernard Janzen, 1992; https://www.youtube.com/watch?v=AffW8rAS5fg

Martin's speculations may be *much more than speculations* when one considers that he was apparently one of a privileged few to read a mysterious prophecy hidden decades ago, deep within the walls of the Vatican—the Third Secret of Fatima! As Martin writes:

In the not too distant future, when the definitive history of the 20th Century has been written, there surely will be universal agreement that the focal point of that century's drama and the key to its meaning for the community of nations, as well as for the salvation of mankind, was an event that took place within the first twenty years of the century, but remained largely unnoticed by the generality of men and women and willfully sidelined by many whose divine vocation it was to announce the advent of Mary's public reign in the history of nations. That keystone event was the Miracle of the Sun on October 13, 1917, at Fatima, in Portugal.[8]

Miracle of the Sun at Fatima

As most devout Catholics are aware, in 1917, amid the horrendous loss of life of World War I, the Blessed Virgin Mary appeared to three shepherd children at Fatima with a plan for peace. On July 13th, the Virgin revealed three secrets to little Lucia and her cousins Jacinta and Francisco, three prophecies regarding the fate of nations and the salvation of souls. The following month, Our Lady promised that on October 13th, she would "perform a miracle so that all may believe."

On that morning, tens of thousands of the faithful flocked to Fatima to witness firsthand the promised miracle, this despite the overt hostility of Portugal's anti-Catholic regime. The crowd of

---

[8] Malachi Martin, foreword, *Fatima Priest*, (Pound Ridge, NY: Good Counsel Publications, 1997), viii.

more than 70,000 people included even avowedly atheist newsmen. This is the testimony of one of them:

> From beside the parked carriages and where many thousands stood, afraid to descend into the muddy soil of the Cova da Iria, we saw the immense crowd turn toward the sun at its highest, free of all clouds. The sun seemed to us like a plate of dull silver. It could be seen without the least effort. It did not blind or burn. It seemed as though an eclipse were taking place. All of a sudden a tremendous shout burst forth, "Miracle, miracle!" Before the astonished eyes of the people, whose attitude carried us back to Biblical times, and who, white with terror, heads uncovered, gazed at the sun which trembled and made brusque and unheard-of movement beyond all cosmic laws, the sun seemed literally to dance in the sky. Immediately afterward the people asked each other if they saw anything and what they had seen. The greatest number avowed that they saw the sun trembling and dancing; others declared they saw the smiling face of the Blessed Virgin herself. They swore that the sun turned around on itself as if it were a wheel of fireworks and had fallen almost to the point of burning the earth with its rays. Some said they saw it change colors successively.[9]

In the months that followed, both Francisco and Jacinta died from the devastating postwar influenza pandemic. In the 1920s, the surviving seer, Lucia Dos Santos, pursued a vocation as a nun. Two decades later, under obedience to her superiors, Lucia composed her memoirs in which she revealed the three "secrets" given by the Virgin to the children:

---

[9] Testimony of Avelino de Almeida in John M. Haffert, *Meet the Witnesses of the Miracle of the Sun*, (Spring Grove, PA: The American Society for the Defense of Tradition, Family and Property, 1961/2006), pp.74-75.

You have seen hell where the souls of poor sinners go. To save them, God wishes to establish in the world devotion to My Immaculate Heart. If what I say to you is done, many souls will be saved and there will be peace. The war is going to end; but if people do not cease offending God, a worse one will break out during the reign of Pius XI. When you see a night illumined by an unknown light, know that this is the great sign given you by God that He is about to punish the world for its sins, by means of war, famine, and persecutions against the Church and of the Holy Father.

To prevent this, I shall come to ask for the Consecration of Russia to My Immaculate Heart, and the Communion of Reparation on the First Saturdays. If My requests are heeded, Russia will be converted, and there will be peace; if not, she will spread her errors throughout the world, causing wars and persecutions of the Church. The good will be martyred, the Holy Father will have much to suffer, various nations will be annihilated...

So the First Secret was a terrifying vision of Hell and an appeal for prayer and penance for poor sinners. The Second was a request for the Pope and all the bishops to consecrate Russia to Mary's Immaculate Heart, in order to prevent the spread of Russia's communist errors causing wars and persecutions, such as World War II. (A request still unfulfilled, as we shall detail in Volume Two.)

The Third Secret, however, was set by the Virgin to be revealed "by 1960 at the latest," but not only was the Secret not disclosed, the seer herself was subsequently censored. As Martin writes:

...in the last third of this [20th] century, there has been such a concerted effort not only to distort the meaning of that keystone event of 1917, but to nullify a divine mandate on which depend the physical safety of millions and the eternal salvation of more millions. The sole surviving person chosen by the Virgin as special witness of the Miracle and the interpreter of its meaning, the 91-year-old Sister Lucia, has been segregated, maligned, misquoted...[10]

It was only two decades later that official sources began to disclose the nature of the Secret without explicitly publishing its content. In 1984, the Prefect of the Vatican's Congregation for the Doctrine of the Faith—none other than Cardinal Joseph Ratzinger —stated in an interview with the magazine *Jesus*:

Yes, I have read it...[The Secret was not revealed] Because, according to the judgement of the Popes, it adds nothing (literally: "nothing different") to what a Christian must know concerning what derives from Revelation: i.e., a radical call for conversion; *the absolute importance of history; the **dangers threatening the faith** and the life of the Christian, and therefore of the world.* And then ***the importance of the 'novissimi' (the last events at the End of Time).*** If it is not made public — at least for the time being — it is in order to prevent religious prophecy from being mistaken for a quest for the sensational (literally: "for sensationalism"). *But the things contained in this "Third Secret" correspond to what has been announced in Scripture and has been said again and again in many other Marian apparitions,* first of all that of Fatima in what is already known of what its message contains. Conversion and penitence are the essential conditions for "salvation".[11]

---

[10] Malachi Martin, *Fatima Priest*, viii.

[11] Vittorio Messori, *Jesus*, Milan (November 11, 1984), pp. 67-81; August 15-18, 1984, Bressanone, Italy.

According to Ratzinger then, the Third Secret speaks (among other things) of the *"novissimi"* what "has been announced in Scripture" concerning the End Times. When we couple this with Martin's statement: "I think [it] is fatally necessary for every Catholic to know…*the fate of the papacy and the coming stress and danger that we shall be without the strength of the papacy,*" we must logically conclude that the Secret alludes to Biblical prophecies of the Days of Antichrist—especially those referring to "being without the strength of the papacy."

St. Paul's 2nd Letter to the Thessalonians, chapter two, may provide just such a reference:

…for that day will not come [Christ's return], unless the rebellion comes first, and the man of lawlessness is revealed, the son of perdition, who opposes and exalts himself against every so-called god or object of worship, so that he takes his seat in the temple of God, proclaiming himself to be God. Do you not remember that when I was still with you, I told you this? And you know *what is restraining [κατέχον]* him now so that he may be revealed in his time. For the mystery of lawlessness is already at work; only *he who now restrains [κατέχων] it will do so until he is out of the way.* And then the lawless one will be revealed, and the Lord Jesus will slay him with the breath of his mouth and destroy him by his appearing and his coming.

The Katechon

In the original Greek grammar, "what is restraining" is a neuter participle and "who now restrains" is a masculine participle. This is odd. Is a neuter "force" holding back the Lawless One, or is it a personal Someone like him? How can it be both? Ratzinger's testimony may be just the interpretive key needed:

Is Peter as a person the [visible] foundation of the Church,[12] or is his profession of faith the foundation of the Church? The answer is: *The profession of faith* [neuter[13]] *exists only as something for which someone is personally responsible* [masculine], and hence the profession of faith is connected with the person. Conversely, the foundation is not a person regarded in a metaphysically neutral way, so to speak, but rather the person as the bearer of the profession of faith— *one without the other would miss the significance of what is meant*...This *personal* liability...forms the heart of the doctrine of *papal primacy*...[14]

Again, in the Greek, the "Katechon" restrains '"until he comes to be out of the middle' or 'out of the midst' (ἐκ μέσου - *ek mesoo*)."[15] Interestingly, Ratzinger refers to the papacy as "the center,"[16] an obstacle against ideological dictatorship:

---

[12] Christ, of course, is the Church's One Foundation.

[13] *"Glaubensbekenntnis"* in Ratzinger's native tongue.

[14] Joseph Ratzinger, "The Primacy of the Pope and the Unity of the People of God," *Communio*, vol 41.1 (September 2014), p. 119.

[15] Stephen Grieve, "Examination of 2 Thessalonians 2:6-7" *Diadems of the Decade* (October 2009), vol 20; http://www.dailycatholic.org/issue/10Oct/102009sg.htm

[16] As does Bishop Vincent Gasser in his *Official Relatio* to the Council Fathers at Vatican I, referring to "the pope, *constituted in the chair of Peter, the center of the Church,*" July 11, 1870; *The Gift of Infallibility: The Official Relatio on Infallibility of Bishop Vincent Ferrer Gasser at Vatican Council I*, Translation James T. O'Connor, 2nd ed. (San Francisco, CA: Ignatius Press, 2008), p. 49.

Many non-Catholics affirm the necessity of a *common* **center** of Christianity. It is becoming evident that *only such a* **center** can be an effective *protection against the drift into dependence on political systems or the pressures emanating from our civilization;* that only by having such *a* **center** can the faith of Christians secure a clear voice in the confusion of ideologies.[17]

In another passage Ratzinger argues even more resolutely:

Abraham, the father of faith, is by his faith the rock that holds back chaos, the onrushing primordial flood of destruction, and thus sustains creation. *Simon,* the first to confess Jesus as the Christ and the first witness of the Resurrection, now becomes by virtue of his Abrahamic *faith, which is renewed in Christ, the rock that stands against the impure tide of unbelief and its destruction of man...*

If it is true that the Successors of St. Peter are—by their nature—Katechons, was Pope Benedict *the* Katechon who was dislodged from "the center" so as to hasten the arrival of the age of Antichrist? Is this why Benedict resigned? And *what* exactly is a "Pope Emeritus"? Are these things foretold in the Third Secret? Will the Church be ruled by an antipope in league with the forces of Antichrist? Has it already begun? And how on earth will the Church ever be able to extricate herself from such a ghastly predicament? The startling answers to these compelling questions will unfold in the ensuing chapters.

---

[17] Joseph Ratzinger, *Called to Communion,* (San Francisco, CA: Ignatius Press, 1996), p. 47.

Chapter One
Katechon: Antidote to Antichrist

"Now concerning the coming of our Lord Jesus Christ and our assembling to meet him, we beg you, brethren, not to be quickly shaken in mind or excited, either by spirit or by word, or by letter purporting to be from us to the effect that the day of the Lord has come. Let no one deceive you in any way; for that day will not come, unless the rebellion comes first, and the man of lawlessness is revealed, the son of perdition, who opposes and exalts himself against every so-called god or object of worship, so that he takes his seat in the temple of God, proclaiming himself to be God. Do you not remember that when I was still with you, I told you this? And you know *what is restraining* him now so that he may be revealed in his time. For the mystery of lawlessness is already at work; only *he who now restrains it will do so until he is out of the way.* And then the lawless one will be revealed, and the Lord Jesus will slay him with the breath of his mouth and destroy him by his appearing and his coming. The coming of the lawless one by the activity of Satan will be with all power and with pretended signs and wonders, and with all wicked deception for those who are to perish, because they refused to love the truth and so be saved. Therefore God sends upon them a strong delusion, to make them believe what is false, so that all may be condemned who did not believe the truth but had pleasure in unrighteousness."

2 Thessalonians 2

St. Paul's audience apparently understood what was restraining the coming era of Antichrist. Not simply what in fact, but *who*: "he who now restrains it will do so until he is out of the way." Leaders of subsequent generations of Christians, however, have had to speculate as to the identity of *what* and *who*.

St. John Chrysostom, Prophet Daniel, and Rome

St. John Chrysostom (c. 347-407), Patriarch of Constantinople and perhaps the greatest of the Eastern Fathers of the Church believed Paul was referring to the Roman Empire:

> ...What then is it that withholdeth, that is, hindereth him [Antichrist] from being revealed? Some indeed say, the grace of the Spirit, but others the Roman empire, to whom I most of all accede. Wherefore? Because if he [Paul] meant to say the Spirit, he would not have spoken obscurely, but plainly...But because he said this of the Roman Empire, he naturally glanced at it, and speaks covertly and darkly. For he did not wish to bring upon himself superfluous enmities, and useless dangers.[18]

St. John argues that if Paul had meant God the Holy Spirit, he would have said so explicitly, but since he references the Restraining force obliquely, it must be the Roman state, the "fall" of which he dare not mention in writing. The first Christians were already viewed as subversives and subjected to accusation and arrest.

John's argument is strengthened by the testimony of a contemporary of Paul, the great Jewish historian Josephus (37-100), who was similarly reticent to refer to Rome's prophetic downfall in his commentary on Daniel: "And Daniel also revealed to the king the meaning of the stone, but I have not thought it proper to relate this, since I am expected to write of what is past and done and not of what is to be."[19] As we shall see, this prophecy of "the Stone" in Daniel 2 seems inextricably bound up with the prophecy of "the Restrainer" in 2 Thessalonians 2.

---

[18] St. John Chrysostom, *Homilies on Second Thessalonians*, IV; As cited in Grieve, http://www.dailycatholic.org/issue/10Oct/102009sg.htm

[19] Josephus, *Jewish Antiquities*, 10. 210 (LCL 6:275).

Nebuchadnezzar (605 – 562 BC), greatest king of the Neo-Babylonian Empire, had a dream which only the Judean Prophet Daniel could interpret for him:

> You saw, O king, and behold, a great image. This image, mighty and of exceeding brightness, stood before you, and its appearance was frightening. The head of this image was of fine gold, its breast and arms of silver, its belly and thighs of bronze, its legs of iron, its feet partly of iron and partly of clay. As you looked, a stone was cut out by no human hand, and it smote the image on its feet of iron and clay, and broke them in pieces; then the iron, the clay, the bronze, the silver, and the gold, all together were broken in pieces, and became like the chaff of the summer threshing floors; and the wind carried them away, so that not a trace of them could be found. But the stone that struck the image became a great mountain and filled the whole earth.
> (Dan. 2:32-35)

Daniel explained that the head of gold was Nebuchadnezzar's own empire, which would be succeeded by three others: those of silver, bronze, and lastly, iron mixed with clay. Josephus confirms for us (though not specifically in his commentary on Daniel 2) that the second or "silver" kingdom represents the Persian Empire, the third or "bronze," the successors of Alexander the Great's Greco-Macedonian Empire, and the fourth "iron" empire, that of Rome.[20] Josephus, however, only free to write by sanction of the imperial family was reluctant to identify the "Stone" Empire destined to smite the Romans, eventually becoming "a great mountain" and "filling the earth." For Josephus, as for other expectant Jews down through the

---

[20] In his comments on Dan 8, which he believed referenced Antiochus IV Epiphanes, he writes: 'In the very same manner [as he wrote of Antiochus IV Epiphanes] Daniel also wrote concerning the Roman government and that our country should be made desolate by them." Ibid., 10. 276.

y

centuries, this was the coming of "the Christ," "the Messiah" whose kingdom would have no end.

The Fathers of the Church were virtually unanimous in their agreement that the fourth kingdom "is that of the Romans;" St. Cyril of Jerusalem confirms that this "has been the tradition of the Church's interpreters."[21] They also agreed that the Stone "not cut by human hands" that strikes the fourth kingdom was none other than Our Lord Jesus Christ: "the Stone which the builders rejected become the cornerstone" (Psalm 118, Matthew 21: 42-44, 1 Peter 2: 4-9).

St. Irenaeus, Tertullian, and St. Cyprian

As St. Irenaeus (130-195) says:

On this account also, Daniel, foreseeing His advent, said that a stone, cut out without hands, came into this world. For this is what 'without hands' means, that His coming into this world was not by the operation of human hands, that is, of those men who are accustomed to stone cutting; that is, Joseph taking no part with regard to it, but Mary alone co-operating with the prearranged plan. For this stone from the earth derives existence from both the power and the wisdom of God. So, then, we understand that His advent in human nature was not by the will of man, but by

---

[21] St. Irenaeus (d. c. 195), the bishop of Lyons, identified the fourth kingdom as "the empire which now rules" in *Against Heresies* 5:26.1., St. Hippolytus (d. 236), presbyter of Rome and author of the first Christian commentary on Daniel wrote: "The legs of iron, and the beast dreadful and terrible expressed the Romans, who hold the sovereignty at present" in *Treatise on Christ and Antichrist* 28. Origen (d. 254), father of biblical studies, in his *Commentary on Genesis* 3.37, Eusebius of Caesarea (d. 339), the father of Church history, in his *Fragmentum Libri* XV (*PG* 22:793), and St. John Chrysostom (d. 407) *Interpretation of the Prophet Daniel* 2. 214 (*PG* 56:206-207) all agree, and St. Jerome (d. 413) wrote in his *Commentary on Daniel* 32: "Now the fourth empire, which clearly refers to the Romans, is the iron empire which breaks in pieces and overcomes all others."

16

the will of God...Christ is the stone which is cut out without hands, who shall destroy temporal kingdoms, and introduce an eternal one, which is the resurrection of the just.[22]

Tertullian (160-220), further elaborates that between the first coming of Christ and his second, he is present to the whole world through his body the Church:

Now these signs of degradation quite suit His first coming, just as the tokens of His majesty do His second advent, when He shall no longer remain "a stone of stumbling and rock of offence," but after His rejection become "the chief corner-stone," accepted and elevated to the top place of the temple, even His church, *being that very stone in Daniel, cut out of the mountain, which was to smite and crush the image of the secular kingdom.*[23]

Or as St. Cyprian (210-258) writes concerning the prophecies of Christ:

That He was to be born of the seed of David after the flesh. That He should be born in Bethlehem. That He should come in lowly condition on His first advent. That He was the righteous One whom the Jews should put to death. That He was called a Sheep and a Lamb who would have to be slain, and concerning the sacrament of the passion. *That He is also called a Stone. That subsequently that stone should become a mountain, and should fill the whole earth. That*

---

[22] St. Irenaeus, *Against Heresies*, 21.7; 5.26.2

[23] Tertullian, *Against Marcion* 3.7 Of this advent the same prophet says: "Behold, one like the Son of man came with the clouds of heaven, and came to the Ancient of days; and they brought Him before Him, and there was given Him dominion and glory, and a kingdom, that all people, nations, and languages should serve Him. His dominion is an everlasting dominion, which shall not pass away; and His kingdom that which shall not be destroyed."

in the last times the same mountain should be manifested, upon which the Gentiles should come, and on which the righteous should go up. That He is the Bridegroom, having the Church as His bride, from whom children should be spiritually born. That the Jews should fasten Him to the cross. That in the passion and the sign of the cross is all virtue and power. That in this sign of the cross is salvation for all who are marked on their foreheads.[24]

St. Augustine

And most clearly, St. Augustine (354-430):

The prophet wishes that by the mountain should be the Jewish kingdom. But the kingdom of the Jews had not filled the whole face of the earth. The stone was cut out from thence, because from thence was the Lord born on His advent among men. And wherefore without hands? Because without the cooperation of man did the Virgin bear Christ...Now then was the stone cut out without hands before the eyes of the Jews, but it was humble. Not without reason; because not yet had that stone increased and filled the whole earth that He showed in His kingdom, which is the Church, with which He has filled the whole face of the earth.[25]

Rome, the fourth kingdom, is to be struck by the Stone not cut by hands and eventually must give way entirely to His Eternal Kingdom. But in between there must be the time of Antichrist, so how do we account for this? For this, we must now return to the exegesis of 2 Thessalonians 2.

---

[24] St. Cyprian, *Testimonies Against the Jews*, Book ii.
[25] St. Augustine, *Tractate 4 on the Gospel of John* 4.4

As we have seen, St. John Chrysostom believed that the Restraining force holding back the reign of Lawlessness was the Roman Empire, which is why St. Paul could not be more precise in his description. St. Augustine also takes up these issues in *The City of God*:

Then as for the words, "And now you know what withholds, i.e., you know what hindrance or cause of delay there is, that he might be revealed in his own time;" they show that he [Paul] was unwilling to make an explicit statement, because he said that they knew. And thus we who have not their knowledge wish and are not able even with pains to understand what the apostle referred to, especially as his meaning is made still more obscure by what he adds. For what does he mean by "For the mystery of iniquity does already work: only he who now holds, let him hold until he be taken out of the way: and then shall the wicked be revealed?" I frankly confess I do not know what he means. I will nevertheless mention such conjectures as I have heard or read.

Some think that the Apostle Paul referred to the Roman empire, and that he was unwilling to use language more explicit, lest he should incur the calumnious charge of wishing ill to the empire which it was hoped would be eternal...it is not absurd to believe that these words of the apostle, "Only he who now holds, let him hold until he be taken out of the way," refer to the Roman empire, as if it were said, "Only he who now reigns, let him reign until he be taken out of the way." And then shall the wicked be revealed: no one doubts that this means Antichrist.[26]

---

[26] St. Augustine, *The City of God*, XX, 19.

Augustine admits that he does not know what or who Paul is talking about, but is willing to entertain the idea that he is speaking of Rome and its emperors. The difficulty is that in the decades *after* Augustine's death (430), Rome definitively *fell* and yet, the Antichrist did not make his appearance. Indeed, it is now 1,600 years later and while there have been many antichrists, *the* Antichrist has yet to show his face.

So here we stand. If Daniel's fourth kingdom is Rome, and if Paul's Restraining force is also Rome, then once Rome falls, we should witness (in quick succession?) the advent of Antichrist followed by the Second Coming of Christ, who "will slay him with the breath of his mouth." But again, it is now the twenty-first century and none of these things has happened?

What if, however, according to Daniel's prophecy, we are still living in "the moment" when the Stone not-made-by-hands struck the fourth kingdom and became a mountain and filled the earth? What if that "moment" has been ongoing for two thousand years?

And furthermore, what if, according to Paul's prophecy, the Restraining force was more than *just* the Roman Empire, but the union of the Roman Empire and Christ's Church/Stone Kingdom as prophesied by Daniel?

This is precisely what the greatest doctor in Church History, St. Thomas Aquinas (1225-1274), argues in his Commentary on 2 Thessalonians:

First comes the revolt...first it is explained as a revolt from the faith because later the faith would be accepted by the whole world...or a revolt of the Roman Empire to which the whole world was subject...but how can this be, since the nations have already withdrawn themselves from the Roman Empire and yet the Antichrist has still not come?

The answer is that it is not over yet but has changed from a temporal revolt into a spiritual revolt as Pope Leo says in a sermon about the Apostles. And so one should say that the revolt from the Roman Empire should be understood not only as a revolt from the temporal but from the spiritual empire namely the Catholic faith of the Roman Church. And it is fitting that as Christ came when the Roman Empire held sway over all, so conversely a sign of Antichrist is revolt against it.[27]

St. Peter, the Rock

Paul's Restrainer had to be living in Paul's day and simultaneously, still living in our own era since Antichrist has not yet come. By the same token, Rome, Daniel's fourth kingdom is not allowed to leave the stage of history before the appearance of Antichrist and the second appearance of Christ. But it has! The only way, therefore, to "save" these joint prophecies is to argue that Rome was transformed by its contact with Christ and the resulting Restraining entity has been faithfully restraining ever since.

This entity, known to Paul in seed form, would not have been clearly observable to the Fathers and Doctors who lived before the fall of Rome, during the time of its embryonic development, but would be quite discernable to us, if we view the Katechon in hindsight as a *transforming union between Roman civilization and the Person of Christ.*

---

[27] St. Thomas Aquinas, *Commentary on the Letters of Saint Paul to the Philippians, Colossians, Thessalonians, Timothy, Titus, and Philemon*, Translation F. R. Larcher, (Lander, WY: Aquinas Institute for the Study of Sacred Doctrine, 2012), pp. 217-218.

Did a Stone, in fact, make contact with Rome in Paul's time? One whose union with Rome created an "entity," a "Restraining force"? A force which came into much greater visibility only after the "decline and fall" of Rome and is still with us today?

The only "thing" that fits this description is the Papacy of the Roman Catholic Church. Or rather, the *union* of the Vicar of Christ ("The Rock") with the City of Rome—*Civitas* here meaning first and foremost the "civilizing" mission of Rome.

Let us look at Christ's commission to Simon "Peter" in Matthew 16 and see how it relates first to Daniel 2 and then to 2 Thessalonians 2. Jesus begins, in fact, by asking the Apostles "Who do men say that the *Son of man* is?" This is a direct reference to his Messianic title from Daniel 7:13.

Now when Jesus came into the district of Caesarea Philippi, he asked his disciples, "Who do men say that the Son of man is?" And they said, "Some say John the Baptist, others say Elijah, and others Jeremiah or one of the prophets." He said to them, "But who do you say that I am?" Simon Peter replied, "You are the Christ, the Son of the living God." And Jesus answered him, "Blessed are you, Simon Bar-Jona! For flesh and blood has not revealed this to you, but my Father who is in heaven. And I tell you, you are Peter, and on this rock, I will build my church, and the gates of hell shall not prevail against it. I will give you the keys of the kingdom of heaven, and whatever you bind on earth shall be bound in heaven, and whatever you loose on earth shall be loosed in heaven." Then he strictly charged the disciples to tell no one that he was the Christ. (Matt. 16:13-20)

Christ took his Apostles the farthest away from home they had ever been when he brought them to Caesarea Philippi at the headwaters of the Jordan River near Israel's Syrian border. The ancient town was called Paneas, after the god Pan, the god of shepherds. King Herod the Great (73 BC – 1 BC) had built a grand temple to the Roman Emperor Augustus (63 BC-AD 14) on this site.

One may understandably ask what must the Jewish Messiah have had in mind by leading his closest followers to such a pagan Gentile location?

The answer is twofold. Firstly, the site is overshadowed by the presence of a tremendous rockface at the foot of which sits a "bottomless" pit (thought to be an entrance to Hell itself). Jesus brought them here

to appoint Peter as the rock. Jesus, the true God of shepherds, appointed Peter as the steward of his kingdom and shepherd of his flock. By choosing this location for the appointment, Jesus clearly shows that he is setting up his divine kingdom in opposition to the worldly kingdom of the Roman Caesars, who claimed divinity for themselves. During the time of Christ, a temple to Caesar Augustus sat at the pinnacle of the rock wall overlooking Caesarea Philippi. In about A.D. 95, Josephus wrote, "So when he [Herod] had conducted Caesar to the sea, and was returned home, he built him a most beautiful temple, of the whitest stone of Zenodorus's country, near the place called Panium. This is a very fine cave in a mountain, under which there is a great cavity in the earth, and the cavern is abrupt, and prodigiously deep, and full of a still water; over it hangs a vast mountain; and under the caverns arise the springs of the river Jordan. Herod adorned this place, which was already a very remarkable one, still further by the erection of this temple, which he dedicated to Caesar" (Josephus, *Jewish Antiquities* 15, 10, 3, in Josephus, *Complete Works*, trans. William Whiston [Grand Rapids, Mich.: Kregel Pub. , 1980], 333). "The epithet ['thou art Peter'] is explained and it is all so much clearer as they stand there before that actual rock which supports the temple dedicated to the lord of the Palatine [Caesar Augustus]. The foundation rock of the spiritual temple which Jesus will build to the Lord of heaven, namely, his Church, is to be the disciple who first declared him the Messias and truly the Son of God." (Giuseppe Ricciotti, *The Life of Christ*, trans. Alba Zizzamia [Milwaukee, Wis.: Bruce Pub. Co. , 1947], 404).[28]

So Simon is called by Christ "Peter," "Rock" while standing in the shadow, not just of any rock—but one dedicated first to the god of shepherds and second to the first living god of the City of Rome, Caesar Augustus. It is as though the Lord is foreshadowing Peter's mission as Shepherd of Christ's flock, Bishop of Rome, *the Rock restraining the Powers of Hell*. In his Ascension, Christ would return to the Father, so he wanted a Vicar to utilize his power here on earth:

Saint Peter bore the divine name of Rock because he represented Christ on earth. This is why Saint Peter and every subsequent Pope receive the title "Vicar of Christ." A vicar is someone who represents another. The term "Vice President" comes from the same Latin word. The Vice President stands in for the President should he be out of the country, in surgery, incapacitated, or even dead. The Vice President is not the President, but he represents him. In the same way, the papal Vicar of Christ is not a divine person, but he does represent a divine Person, that is, Our Lord

[28] Stephen K. Ray, *Upon This Rock*, (San Francisco, CA: Ignatius Press, 1999), pp. 32-33, Nt. 32.

Jesus Christ. Peter and all successive Popes are not literally the Rock of Salvation spoken of by Old Testament writers. However, Christ appointed them to represent Him in that way, and so He built His Church upon this special office...[29]

We know that Jesus meant to make Simon his Vicar, not merely by calling him "Rock," but by promising him "the keys." This is a reference to Isaiah 22 wherein God speaks of replacing a corrupt vicar of the King of Israel with a new one:

Thus says the Lord God of hosts, "Come, go to this steward, to Shebna, who is over the household, and say to him: What have you to do here, and whom have you here, that you have hewn here a tomb for yourself, you who hew a tomb on the height, and carve a habitation for yourself in the rock? Behold, the Lord will hurl you away violently, O you strong man. He will seize firm hold on you, and whirl you round and round, and throw you like a ball into a wide land; there you shall die, and there shall be your splendid chariots, you shame of your master's house. I will thrust you from your office, and you will be cast down from your station. In that day I will call my servant Eliakim the son of Hilkiah, and I will clothe him with your robe, and will bind your girdle on him, and will commit your authority to his hand; and he shall be a father to the inhabitants of Jerusalem and to the house of Judah. *And I will place on his shoulder the key of the house of David; he shall open, and none shall shut; and he shall shut, and none shall open. And I will fasten him like a peg in a sure place, and he will become a throne of honor to his father's house.* And they will hang on him the whole weight of his father's house, the offspring and issue, every small vessel, from the cups to all the flagons. *In that*

[29] Taylor Marshall, *Eternal City*, (St. John Press, 2012) Kindle Edition.

day, says the Lord of hosts, the peg that was fastened in a sure place will give way; and it will be cut down and fall, and the burden that was upon it will be cut off, for the Lord has spoken." (Isaiah 22:15-25)

Shebna's (c 700s BC) power, symbolized by "the key" of the Davidic Kingship is to be given to a more worthy recipient, namely Eliakim. And whatever "he shall open...none shall shut" and what "he shall shut...none shall open." This passage is clearly what Christ had in mind when he tells Peter: "I will give you the keys of the kingdom of heaven, and whatever you bind on earth shall be bound in heaven, and whatever you loose on earth shall be loosed in heaven."

And yet, Isaiah adds enigmatically, that "in that day" God will allow even "the peg that was fastened in a sure place" to "give way; and it will be cut down and fall, and the burden that was upon it will be cut off." Biblical commentators have been puzzled why this fate should befall Eliakim which had previously befallen Shebna? The force of the contrast between them would be lost if he ended up with the same fate as his predecessor.

But since Matthew invites us to read this Old Testament passage in light of the New, one wonders if this last line of Isaiah is not also a prediction regarding the papacy as were the previous ones? In other words, could *"In that day, says the Lord of hosts, the peg that was fastened in a sure place will give way"* be the equivalent of "And you know what is restraining him now so that he may be revealed *in his time...*only he who now restrains it will do so until *he is out of the way.*" from 2 Thessalonians 2? The Rock of Peter, like the Peg of Eliakim will bear weight, will hold fast indeed, until the appointed time of Lawlessness. Note that Christ promised that the powers of death would not prevail against his Church—no explicit guarantee is made for the Rock upon which it rests!

26

Christ gives Simon the office of Vicar. He calls him Peter, that is, "Rock" because he and his successors will function in Christ's place until the era of his second coming. It was foretold by Daniel:

According to the Prophet Daniel, "the God of heaven will set up a kingdom," by sending forth a "stone" to break up the Fourth Kingdom, which is Rome. That stone shall become, "a great mountain and fill the whole earth" (Dan 2:35). When Christ appoints Simon as Peter the Rock and gives him the keys of the Kingdom, He is effectively saying that Daniel's prophecy concerning the coming of the Son of Man during the reign of the Fourth Kingdom is being fulfilled. The entire episode of Peter receiving the keys of the kingdom begins with Christ's question, "Who do men say that the Son of man is?" (Mt 16:13). Daniel identifies "the Son of Man" with the era of the Fourth Kingdom (Dan 7:13, 19).[30]

St. Peter, Bishop of Rome

Not only did Peter become Vicar of Christ during the time of the fourth kingdom, but he also established himself in the very capital of that empire. Biblical and historical sources confirm his Roman presence beyond a reasonable doubt. First the biblical evidence:

Sometime around the year A.D. 42, Herod Agrippa [of Judea] murdered Saint James the Greater and imprisoned Saint Peter in order to appease the Jewish leadership of Jerusalem (Acts 12). Peter escaped from prison through the miraculous intervention of an angel. The narrative ends with Peter escaping to an unnamed location. "Then he

---

[30] Ibid., p. 75.

departed and went to another place" (Acts 12:17). Catholic tradition affirms that Peter's departure to "another place" was in fact an anonymous reference to Peter's first visit to Rome in A.D. 42. The identification of Rome as the anonymous location of Peter's whereabouts between 42 and 49 would explain several historical mysteries. First, the Book of Acts depicts Peter as being entirely absent from Jerusalem between the years A.D. 42 and 49. Second, it would explain the Jewish riots that occurred in Rome and eventually led to the Edict of Claudius in A.D. 49...

In A.D. 49 the Emperor Claudius expelled all Jews from the city of Rome. Not a single Jew was allowed to remain in the city. The Roman historian Suetonius provides us with the reason. Suetonius records that the Roman Jews engaged in continual riots insinuated by "Chrestus their ringleader." There is no other historical record of a Roman Jew named "Chrestus." The Roman authorities knew only that some Jews united around "Chrestus," and some Jews were bitterly opposed to "Chrestus." The debate had become publicly dangerous! If Peter had been in Rome during this time, it would explain why the Jews became so riotous—not over a controversial Roman Jew named Chrestus but over a resurrected Jew named Christus. Many have suggested that the Roman authorities expelled the Jewish population of Rome because the Jews had become so embattled over the person and claims of Christus, that is, the Christ and King of the Jews. The name "Chrestus" is therefore a Roman mispronunciation of the title "Christus."[31]

In addition, we have the testimony of Paul in his Letter to the Romans:

---

[31] Ibid., p. 81.

Paul further explains why he has not yet come to Rome: "I make it my ambition to preach the gospel, not where Christ has already been named, lest I build on the foundation of another man" (Rom 15:20-21). The implication is that Paul has no need to come to Rome because "another man" has already built the foundation of the Church in Rome. The sufficiency of this other man's Apostleship is manifest by Paul's doctrine that the Apostles are the only men capable of laying the foundation of the Church in Christ (Gal 1:11-24). Thus, Paul had no desire to establish the Church in Rome because he saw the Church of Rome as perfectly established by "another man" with Apostolic credentials. Tradition identifies this "other man" as none other than Peter himself. This would explain the rather obscure reason given by Paul for his being "hindered very much" from coming to Rome (Rom 15:22). Paul was aware of his controversial status in the Church. If the Jews of Rome were rioting because of Peter, Paul would have driven them into hysteria! It would not have been appropriate for Paul to go to Rome. Paul's affirmation that Rome is fully established under Apostolic authority is seen in his desire merely "to pass through" Rome and "enjoy your company for a little" as he travels to Spain (Rom 15:24).[32]

Peter fled Rome but would return after the death of Claudius (AD 55) and the repeal of his expulsion of the Jews (AD 56). We have a letter from Peter himself that proves this:

In his First Epistle, Peter sends his greetings from the Church "in Babylon" (1 Pet 5:13). Scholars are in agreement that Babylon was often used as a code word for Rome. For example, the Apocalypse of Saint John and the Sibylline Oracles (5:143, 159) both use the term "Babylon" to denote

---

[32] Ibid., p. 86.

the city of Rome. The reason should be obvious. Rome was the fourth stage of the evil empire beginning with the first kingdom of Babylon. Rome was the heir of the savage political power that made war against Israel.[33]

Historical and archeological evidence also bears witness to the Roman Pastorship of Peter.

Dionysius of Corinth [d. 171] wrote: "You have thus by such an admonition bound together the plantings of Peter and Paul at Rome and Corinth." Here Dionysius confirms that Peter and Paul "planted" the Church at Rome, and that Pope Soter had bound Corinth by his commands. The mention of "binding" no doubt refers to Saint Peter's binding on heaven and earth, as mentioned by Christ in Matthew 16:19...

Tertullian, writing around the year 218, speaks of "those whom Peter baptized in the Tiber River." The Tiber River is of course the waterway running along the western side of Rome. Tertullian also writes, "How happy is its church, on which Apostles poured forth all their doctrine along with their blood! Where Peter endured a passion like that of the Lord, where Paul was crowned in a death like that John [the Baptist]."

Origen of Alexandria, writing around A.D. 230 records that Peter, "having finally come to Rome, was crucified head-downwards, because he had requested that he might suffer this way."

St. John Chrysostom wrote: "I love Rome even for this, although indeed one has other grounds for praising it, both for its greatness, and its antiquity, and its beauty, and its population, and for its power, and its wealth, and for its successes in war. But I let

---

[33] Ibid.

all this pass, and esteem it blessed on this account, that both in Peter's lifetime he wrote to them, and loved them so, and talked with them whiles he was with us, and brought his life to a close there."[34]

When Paul wrote the Thessalonians a second letter to calm their fears of an impending end of the world, it would have been most imprudent indeed to explicitly mention Rome or Peter. What was clear to Paul would have been less so for future commentators, however, precisely due to his circumlocutions. Nevertheless, we who have the benefit of two thousand years of hindsight are better equipped to unpack the enigma of the Katechon.

---

[34] St. John Chrysostom, *Homily 32 on Romans*.

Chapter Two
Pope Benedict:
"Taken Out of the Center"[35]

"A Pope Emeritus is impossible." [36]
Blessed Pope John Paul II, 2002

"For some theologians **the Papacy is a sacrament**. *The Germans are very creative in all these things.* I do not think so, but I want to say that it is something special."[37]
Pope Francis/Jorge Bergoglio, 2015

"[M]edieval doctrine...not only differentiated but professed full separation of the [following] two realities...only power of order derives from episcopal ordination, whereas the source of all forms of jurisdiction is exclusively the papal office. In consequence of this (sacramentally inaccurate) starting point, jurisdictional power assumed a one-sidedly 'vertical' character in the medieval ecclesiological model. *This deviation would be corrected only in the second half of the last century thanks to the recognition that* ***ecclesiastical power (as sacred reality) is in its entirety of sacramental origin.*** *As Mörsdorf emphasised after the Council "order and jurisdiction cannot be considered two separate powers but complementary elements of the one ecclesiastical power".* ***Thus, governing power ('jurisdiction') also derives from episcopal ordination..."***
Péter Szabo

---

[35] Parts of this chapter are taken from my peer-reviewed journal article: "What Ratzinger Renounced and What is Irrevocable in Pope Emeritus," *Archivio Giuridico di Filippo Serafini*, CLIV, no. 3 (2022), pp. 721-751.

[36] John Paul II to Lord Conrad Black, during 2002 papal visit to Canada; as cited http://katholisches.info/2016/06/21/johannes-paul-ii-ein-emeritierter-papst-ist-unmoeglich/

[37]http://www.archivioradiovaticana.va/storico/2015/03/13/ pope_francis_on_his_pontificate_to_date/en-1129074

"The most crucial event in the development of the Latin West was, I think, the increasing distinction between sacrament [*potestas ordinis*] and jurisdiction [*potestas iurisdictionis*], between liturgy and administration as such... I think we should be honest enough to admit the temptation of mammon in the history of the Church and to recognize to what extent it was a real power that worked to the *distortion and corruption of both Church and theology, even to their inmost core. The separation of office as jurisdiction from office as rite* was continued *for reasons of prestige and financial benefits."*
Cardinal Joseph Ratzinger, 1982

"[H]e has not abandoned the Office of Peter—something which would have been entirely impossible for him after his irrevocable acceptance of the office in April 2005. By an act of extraordinary courage, he has instead renewed this office. Since February 2013 the papal ministry is therefore no longer what it was before."
Archbishop Georg Gänswein, 2016

Only one month after Pope Benedict announced his renunciation of the ministry of the Bishop of Rome, Italian philosopher Massimo Cacciari stated:

The Church has also always been characterized by its ability to "hold back", [Katechon] to halt—as we read in Saint Paul—the advance of the anti-Christ forces. We must therefore ask ourselves whether Ratzinger's decision is not a lucid declaration of impotence to support a function of "power that holds back"...We could hypothesize that Ratzinger resigns because he is no longer able to contain the anti-Christic powers, *within the Church itself.* As Augustine said, the antichrists are in us. This is a key to Ratzinger's decision, if we are to read it in all its seriousness...The Church is faced, for the first time, with the true essence of the antichrist.[38]

Did Ratzinger's resignation spell the end of the restraint of the forces of Antichrist? Was the Katechon finally "taken out of the center"? It is crucial that we understand what Ratzinger renounced and what was irrevocable (to his mind) in "Pope Emeritus." In fact, an intensive investigation of Ratzinger's thoughts may reveal that his resignation was not valid after all, and that consequently, Jorge Bergoglio is no more pope than you or I.

"Elementary, my Dear Watson"

Let us imagine a body found in a room which was locked from the inside. Why engage in such a morbid thought experiment? Because sometimes murder mysteries are apt analogies for sacred mysteries.

2010 saw the return to British television of the world's most famous private detective—Sherlock Holmes. And in one of the premiere episodes of *Sherlock*, the police find a gunshot victim holding a gun inside a locked room. They naturally assume, therefore, that it is suicide. But Sherlock protests:

SHERLOCK: Wrong. [Suicide] It's one *possible* explanation of *some* of the facts. You've got a solution that you like, but you're choosing to ignore anything you see that doesn't comply with it.

It is the same way with those who admit no possibility that Pope Benedict XVI resigned invalidly. They have a surface-level

---

[38] Marco Dotti, "Cacciari: il nuovo Papa dovrà sfidare l'Anticristo," *Vita* (March 11, 2013); http://www.vita.it/it/article/2013/03/11/cacciari-il-nuovo-papa-dovra-sfidare-lanticristo/122928/; My translation from the Italian.

solution that they like and they are choosing to ignore anything that can be seen that doesn't comply with it. Author and blogger Steven O'Reilly, for example, states categorically: "there is no reason or evidence...that should lead one to reject the validity of Pope Benedict's resignation."[39]

Let's return to our corpse case:

SHERLOCK: The wound was on the *right* side of his head.
INSPECTOR DIMMOCK: And?
SHERLOCK: Van Coon was left-handed. *(He goes into an elaborate mime as he demonstrates his point, pretending to try and point a gun to his right temple with his left hand.)* Requires quite a bit of contortion.
INSPECTOR DIMMOCK: Left-handed?
SHERLOCK: Coffee table on the left-hand side; coffee mug handle pointing to the left. Power sockets: habitually used the ones on the left...Pen and paper on the left-hand side of the phone because he picked it up with his right and took down messages with his left. D'you want me to go on?...: *(pointing towards the kitchen)* There's a knife on the breadboard with butter on the right side of the blade because he used it with his left.
(He turns to Dimmock with an impatient look on his face.)
SHERLOCK: It's highly unlikely that a left-handed man would shoot himself in the *right* side of his head. Conclusion: someone broke in here and murdered him. *Only* explanation of *all* the facts.[40]

---

[39] Steven O'Reilly, "Benedict is NOT pope," *Roma Locuta Est* (September 4, 2017); https://romalocutaest.com/2017/09/04/benedict-is-not-pope/

[40] *Sherlock*, Season 1, episode 2 transcript: "The Blind Banker," part 1 Episode written by Steve Thompson; Transcript by Ariane DeVere aka Callie Sullivan; https://arianedevere.livejournal. com/45111.html

In the case of Pope Benedict's renunciation and transformation into Pope Emeritus, a conclusion that explains all of the facts must answer all of these questions: Why did Benedict XVI choose to become "Pope Emeritus" instead of returning to being Cardinal Ratzinger, especially when there is currently no such office in canon law—nor in the Church's two-thousand-year history? Why did he still issue Apostolic Blessings in his own name when only a pope can do that? Why was his proper form of address still "His Holiness" when only a pope can be called that? And why did he choose to continue wearing papal white? Could it truly be for his stated reason—absurd on its face—"there were no black cassocks available in Rome" at the time?[41] And why was it that every time the putative pope created new cardinals at consistories, he always presented them to "His Holiness" Benedict XVI?

Like Sherlock Holmes, it's time to dig deeper.

Ratzinger Renounces (ONLY) the *Active* Ministry

In his last General Audience of Wednesday February 27, 2013, Pope Benedict provided his own interpretation of his Declaration of Resignation of February 11th:

In these last months I have felt my energies declining, and I have asked God insistently in prayer to grant me his light...I have taken this step with full awareness of its gravity and *even its novelty*, but with profound interior serenity...

---

[41] "I continue to wear the white cassock and kept the name Benedict for purely practical reasons. At the moment of my resignation there were no other clothes available. In any case, I wear the white cassock in a visibly different way to how the Pope wears it. This is another case of completely unfounded speculations being made." Ratzinger's (alleged) written reply to Andrea Tornielli; https://www.lastampa.it/vatican-insider/en/2014/02/28/news/ratzinger-my-resignation-is-valid-speculations-are-simply-absurd-1.35928994

Here, allow me to go back once again to _19 April 2005_. The real gravity of the decision was also due to the fact that from **that moment on I was engaged always and forever by the Lord. Always—anyone who accepts the Petrine ministry no longer has any privacy.** He belongs always and completely to everyone, to the whole Church...

The "always" is also a "forever" –there is no longer a return to the private. _My decision to renounce the active exercise of the ministry does not revoke this._ I do not return to private life, to a life of travel, meetings, receptions, conferences, etc. I do not abandon the cross but remain in a new way with the Crucified Lord. _I no longer carry the power of the [Petrine] office for the government_ of the Church, but _in the service of prayer I remain, so to speak, in the precincts of St. Peter._ Saint Benedict, whose name I bear as Pope, will be a great example to me in this. He has shown us the way to a life, which, **active or passive,** belongs totally to the work of God.[42]

In the first place—and this cannot be overemphasized—Benedict states that his renunciation of the Papacy is a _qualified_ one. "Anyone who accepts the Petrine ministry" is engaged by it so that his "decision to renounce the _active_ exercise of the ministry does not revoke this," does not revoke the passive exercise, the Petrine ministry in its ontological dimension. This is perfectly consistent with Ratzinger's onetime remark: "We have no right to speak of a quasi-profane ruling power, _neatly separated from the sacramental ministry._"[43]

---

[42] https://www.vatican.va/content/benedict-xvi/en/audiences/2013/documents/hf_ben-xvi_aud_20130227.html; Full text in Appendix IV.

[43] Joseph Ratzinger, _Theological Highlights of Vatican II_, (New York/Mahwah, New Jersey: Paulist Press, 1966), p. 128.

Sensational headlines were made in December 2022, when the national director of Priests For Life, Fr. Frank Pavone, was stripped of his priestly faculties by Pope Francis. Although he is now prohibited from engaging in the "active" ministry of a priest (offering the Holy Sacrifice of the Mass, hearing Confessions, etc.), nevertheless, passively he remains "a priest forever according to the Order of Melchizedek" (Heb. 7:17). Benedict was claiming the same ontological reality for himself: stripped of practical power, he was now a passive pope—but pope nonetheless! This is undoubtedly the "novelty" to which Ratzinger refers.

Then we have the added testimony of Archbishop Georg Gänswein, Benedict's "right hand" for two decades. In a 2016 speech at the Gregorianum, Gänswein said that unlike the resignation of Pope St. Celestine which *changed __him__* back into the humble monk Pietro Morrone, in the case of the resignation of Pope Benedict, "the *__papal ministry__ is…no longer what it was before*":

> I was present when…he [Benedict] decided *not to give up the name he had chosen*, as Pope Celestine V had done when, on December 13, 1294, a few months after the start of his ministry, he again became Pietro dal Morrone.
>
> *Since February 2013 the papal ministry is therefore no longer what it was before.* It is and remains the foundation of the Catholic Church; and yet it is a foundation which *Benedict XVI has profoundly and permanently transformed* during his exceptional pontificate (*Ausnahmepontifikat*)…

He calls Benedict's status since 2013 a "pontificate." Indeed:

> [Benedict] has been *daring enough* to open the door to a new phase, to that historical turning point which no one…could

39

have ever imagined. Since then, we live in an historic era which in the *2,000-year history of the Church is without precedent.* Many people even today continue to see this new situation as a kind of **exceptional (not regular) state of the divinely instituted** *office of Peter* (*eine Art göttlichen Ausnahmezustandes*) ...

But in the history of the Church it shall remain true that, in the year 2013, the famous theologian on the throne of Peter became *history's first "pope emeritus."* Since then, *his role—* allow me to repeat it once again—*is entirely different* from that, for example, of the holy Pope Celestine V.[44]

Pope Emeritus means "Pope without an Active See"

Benedict applied the conciliar innovation of "bishop emeritus"[45] to the bishop of Rome. As we shall see,[46] the ecclesiology of the Council did away with the notion of a bishop having "legitimacy" only through papal sanctioned office, e.g. "Bishop of Milan." As Ratzinger once wrote:

---

[44] Diane Montagna's Translation, reproduced in Appendix V: https://aleteia.org/2016/05/30/complete-english-text-archbishop-georg-gansweins-expanded-petrine-office-speech/; "We, Celestine, Pope V, moved by legitimate reasons, that is to say, for the sake of humility, of a better life and an unspotted conscience, of weakness of body and of want of knowledge, the malignity of the people, and personal infirmity, recover the tranquility and consolation of our former life, *do freely and voluntarily resign the pontificate, the place, the dignity, occupation, and honors of which we expressly renounce,* and we give full and free faculty to the college of cardinals canonically to elect a pastor of the Universal Church." Translation Artaud de Montor, *The Lives and Times of the Popes,* vol. 3, (New York: Catholic Publication Society of America, 1911).

[45] An ecclesiastical office, which by its nature lacks the power of jurisdiction (Cf. Can. 402 §1); its status is defined in Chapter IX of the *Directory Apostolorum successores;* https://www.vatican.va/roman_curia/congregations/cbishops/documents/rc_con_cbishops_doc_20040222_apostolorum-successores_en.html; Cf. also Congregatione Per I Vescovi, *Il Vescovo Emerito,* (Vatican City: Libreria Editrice Vaticana, 2008).

[46] Cf. Appendix I and forthcoming Vol. II of *The Third Secret of Fatima and the Synodal Church.*

The most crucial event in *the development of the Latin West* was, I think, the increasing distinction between sacrament [*potestas ordinis*] and jurisdiction [*potestas iurisdictionis*], between liturgy and administration as such...

I think we should be honest enough to admit the temptation of mammon in the history of the Church and to recognize to what extent it was a real power that worked to the *distortion and corruption of both Church and theology, even to their inmost core. The separation of office as jurisdiction from office as rite was continued for reasons of prestige and financial benefits.*[47]

In giving up the "office as jurisdiction," in this case, the administration of the diocese of Rome—and the universal Church —Benedict was *not* parting with the "office as rite."[48] To return to being "Cardinal Ratzinger" would have been tantamount to denying the interpenetration of the functional and the sacramental, as he says: *"both the sacrament and the 'ruling power' interpenetrate one another."*[49] Thus he remained "pope" in the sense that a bishop remains a "bishop" even without a diocese to run:

This word *"emerito"* meant that he was no longer the *active holder of the episcopal see*, but that he had the special relationship of a former bishop to his see. In this respect, on the one hand, the need to *define his office* [as rite] in relation to a real diocese without making him a second bishop of his diocese was taken into account. The word

---

[47] Joseph Ratzinger, *Principles of Catholic Theology: Building Stones for a Fundamental Theology*, Translation M. F. McCarthy, (San Francisco, CA: Ignatius Press, 1987), pp. 254-256.

[48] One may retire from the active or "Martha" dimension of the Petrine Ministry, but not the "Mary." dimension, which in the end, "is the one thing necessary." Cf. Lk 10:38-42.

[49] Ratzinger, *Theological Highlights*, p. 128.

"*emerito*" meant that he had fully relinquished his office [as jurisdiction], but the *spiritual attachment* [office as rite] to his previous see was now also recognized as a legal quality...*This relationship to a preceding see, which had hitherto been real, but which was seen as outside the realm of law is the new meaning of "emerito" formed after Vatican II*. It does not create any participation in the concrete legal [jurisdictional] content of the episcopal [diocesan] office, but at the same time sees the *spiritual bond as a reality*. Thus, there are not two bishops [of the diocese], but there is *a spiritual mission* [i.e. *munus* as rite], *whose essence is to serve from within*, from the Lord, in prayerful being with and for his previous diocese...no concrete legal [jurisdictional] authority anymore, but a *spiritual assignment*, which remains—even if *invisible*. Precisely this [now] legal-*spiritual form* [office as rite] avoids any thought of a coexistence of two [reigning] popes: a bishop's see can have only one holder. At the same time, *a spiritual bond* is expressed *that cannot be taken away under any circumstances*.[50]

To Benedict's mind, the situation was not a "coexistence of two [reigning] popes: a bishop's see can have only one holder." That is, he defines "Pope," conventionally speaking as the "Bishop of Rome," the active holder of the diocese of Rome. In that sense, both Benedict and Gänswein considered Francis "the Pope." Journalist and author Paul Badde interviewed Gänswein just weeks after his May 2016 speech and Gänswein referred to *Francis* as

the lawfully elected and lawful pope. That is to say, there are not two popes—the one lawful, the other unlawful, that

---

[50] Peter Seewald, *Benedikt XVI.: Ein Leben*, "Letzte Fragen an Benedikt XVI," (Munich: Droemer, 2020); My translation from the German.

is simply not correct. And I simply said [May 2016]—that is also what Pope Benedict said [February 2013]—that he, after all, is still present with his prayers, with his sacrifices, in the *"Recinto"* of Saint Peter [within the walls and precincts of the Vatican], and that, through these prayers, through these sacrifices, there shall come forth spiritual fruit for his successors and for the Church. [51]

Nevertheless, Gänswein considered Benedict a present successor of Peter—not a former one—and thus, in that sense he added: "now [2016] we have had for three years *two popes* and I have the impression that the reality that I perceive is covered by what I have said."[52] Gänswein does not mince words: Benedict has remained pope [in some sense] for the three years since his exit. Indeed, Benedict, himself, claimed that a *papal bond* still adhered to his soul "that cannot be taken away under any circumstances."

This means that he did not renounce the papacy in its entirety.

How do we know that Benedict's "spiritual bond" was *"papal?"* Because he claimed a bond with the see of Rome and the see of Rome is the Apostolic See, the papal see.

This is exactly how Badde understands Gänswein—and the Archbishop, himself, confirms it:

Badde: "If I understand you aright, *he [Benedict] remained in the office*, but in the contemplative part [office as rite],

---

[51] Paul Badde, "Exklusives Interview mit Erzbischof Georg Gänswein," *Rom direkt* EWTN Germany (June 27, 2016); https://www.youtube.com/watch?v=3jyZ8CRllR0; Cf. https://www.ncregister. com/blog/english-transcript-of-archbishop-gaensweins-ewtn-germany-interview

[52] Ibid.

without having any authority to decide [office as jurisdiction]. Thus we have – as you said – now an active and a contemplative part which form together an enlargement of the *Munus Petrinum* [primacy and office of Peter]?"

Gänswein: *"That is what I have said, indeed..."*

The "Petrine *Munus*": Active vs. Passive Ministry

Returning to his Last Audience, Ratzinger reminds the faithful that his renunciation of the active ministry "does not revoke" his original *papal commitment* of April 19, 2005, which is ongoing: "always and forever." He is giving up the active "power of the [Petrine] office for the government" of the diocese of Rome and the universal Church, but not the passive power of the [Petrine] office denoted by the Cross and by prayer. In an address he gave in 1977, Ratzinger says:

The office of the papacy is a cross, indeed, the greatest of all crosses. For what can be said to pertain more to the cross and anxiety of the soul than the care and [personal] responsibility for all the Churches...attachment to the Word and will of God because of the Lord is what makes the *sedes* [Chair/Throne] a cross and thus proves the Vicar [the Pope] to be a representative [of Christ].[53]

Also in his Last Audience, Ratzinger reiterates that his sufferings and prayers are indeed *papal*: "I remain, so to speak, in

---

[53] Joseph Ratzinger, October 1977, Symposium Address "On the Nature and Commission of the Petrine Ministry" marking the 80th birthday of Pope Paul VI; Cf. "The Primacy of the Pope and the unity of the People of God," "Der Primat des Papstes und die Einheit des Gottesvolkes" in Ratzinger Editor, *Dienst an der Einheit* (*Service to Unity*), (Patmos, 1978); it has also been republished in books by Ignatius Press and in *Communio* (Spring 2014).

the precincts of St. Peter." (Not "so to speak" at all, but very *matter of fact*—Benedict never left the Vatican!)

His namesake, St. Benedict, has taught him that being a Holy Father is not simply *"labora,"* but, more importantly, *"ora"*[54]!

As Gänswein says of Benedict's novel renunciation:

> It was "the least expected step in contemporary Catholicism," [Benedict biographer] Regoli writes, and yet a possibility which Cardinal Ratzinger had already pondered publicly on August 10, 1978, in Munich, in a homily on the occasion of the death of Paul VI. *Thirty-five years later, he has not abandoned the Office of Peter— something which would have been entirely impossible for him after his irrevocable acceptance of the office in April 2005.*

Thus Benedict's proper form of address was still "His Holiness." He still issued Apostolic Blessings *in his own name.* He still wore white. And still resided in the Vatican. An unprecedented situation which troubled more than a few, for almost a decade:

> If the pope who resigns from the pontificate retains the title of *emeritus, that means that to some extent he remains pope.* It is clear, in fact, that in the definition the noun [pope] prevails over the adjective [*emeritus*]. But why is he still pope after the abdication? The only explanation possible is that the pontifical election has imparted an indelible character, which he does not lose with the resignation. The abdication would presuppose in this case the cessation of the exercise of power, but not the disappearance of the pontifical character. This indelible character attributed to the pope

---

[54] Famous maxim of St. Benedict: *"Ora et Labora;"* "Prayer and Work."

could be explained in its turn only by *an ecclesiological vision that would subordinate the juridical dimension [potestas iurisdictionis] of the pontificate to the sacramental [potestas ordinis]*.[55]

Unsettling as all this "novelty" may be to some, none of it should surprise us. Already in his February 11th *Declaratio*, Benedict qualified what the Petrine office (*munus* in Latin) is and what he was (and what he was not) renouncing in connection to it:

After having repeatedly examined my conscience before God, I have come to the certainty that my strengths, due to an advanced age, are no longer suited to an adequate *exercise* of the *Petrine munus*.

I am well aware that this *munus, due to its essential spiritual nature*, must be **carried out** not only with words and deeds, but *no less with prayer and suffering*.[56]

Conscientia mea iterum atque iterum coram Deo explorata ad cognitionem certam perveni vires meas ingravescente aetate non iam aptas esse ad munus Petrinum aeque administrandum.
Bene conscius sum hoc munus secundum suam essentiam spiritualem non solum agendo et loquendo exsequi debere, sed non minus patiendo et orando.

For Benedict, the Petrine *munus*, in its essence is "spiritual," not "functional." It is an ontological "always," a "forever" that

---

[55] Roberto de Mattei, "One and One Alone is Pope," quoted in "Reigning and 'Emeritus.' The Enigma of the Two Popes," *Chiesa Espresso* [Sandro Magister's Blog] (September 15, 2014); http://chiesa.espresso. repubblica.it/articolo/1350868bdc4.html?eng=y Cf. Appendix I.

[56] https://www.vatican.va/content/benedict-xvi/en/speeches/2013/february/documents/hf_ben-xvi_spe_20130211_declaratio.html; Full text in English and Latin in Appendix III.

cannot be revoked. So again, Ratzinger's renunciation was qualified:

> *I renounce the ministry of the Bishop of Rome*, Successor of Saint Peter, entrusted to me by the Cardinals on 19 April 2005, in such a way, that as from 28 February 2013, at 20:00 hours, the See of Rome, the See of Saint Peter, will be vacant and a Conclave to elect the new Supreme Pontiff will have to be convoked by those whose competence it is.

> *declaro me ministerio Episcopi Romae, Successoris Sancti Petri, mihi per manus Cardinalium die 19 aprilis MMV commisso renuntiare ita ut a die 28 februarii MMXIII, hora 20, sedes Romae, sedes Sancti Petri vacet et Conclave ad eligendum novum Summum Pontificem ab his quibus competit convocandum esse.*

In the first quote from the *Declaratio* reproduced above, Benedict uses *"munus Petrinum"* to describe the essential spiritual nature of the "Petrine ministry;" he is able to fulfill this *"munus"* through suffering and prayer, but is no longer able to do so through words and deeds.

Why then, may we ask, did he suddenly replace *"munus"* with *"ministerio"* in the last quote? Why abandon the consistency of his narration? More importantly, why abruptly change from speaking of the "Petrine" ministry or *"munus Petrinum,"* to the more restricted: *"ministerio Episcopi Romae,"* "ministry of the *Bishop of Rome"* instead?

His *Declaratio*: "I renounce the ministry of the Bishop of Rome" is, in fact, quite consistent with what he said in his Last Audience: "I no longer carry the power of the [Petrine] office for the government of the Church ["words and deeds"], but in the service of prayer I remain, so to speak, in the precincts of St. Peter [Petrine *munus*]."

As Stefano Violi, Professor of Canon Law in the Theological Faculty of Emilia-Romagna observes:

In the cited passage Benedict XVI proposes two fundamental distinctions in the order of the Petrine *munus*: in the first place he distinguishes *munus* [office] from *executio muneris* [execution of office]...[I]n the second place, he distinguishes between the different activities which accompany the *executio*, between an administrative-ministerial *executio* (*agendo* and *loquendo* [acting and speaking]) and a more spiritual one (*orando* and *patiendo* [praying and suffering or endurance])...Seeing his own incapacity **to administer** the goods of the ministry entrusted to him, **he declared his renunciation from the ministerium. Not from the papacy**, *according to the dictate of the norm of Boniface VIII;* **not from the munus** *according to the dictate of can. 332 § 2,* but from the *ministerium,* or, as he will specify in his last audience, from "the **active exercise** of the ministry."

The service to the Church continues with the same love and the same dedication, although outside the exercise of power. **The object of the irrevocable resignation, in fact, is the executio muneris (execution of the office) by speaking and acting** (*agendo et loquendo*) **not the munus [office] entrusted to him once and forever.**[57]

[57] Stefano Violi, "The Resignation of Benedict XVI: Between History, Law and Conscience," *Rivista teologica di Lugano,* XVIII (February 2013), pp. 155-166; Cf. *Decretum Gratiani,* c. 24, q. 1, dict. post. c. 37; https://web.archive.org/web/20150315063401/http://www.fatima.org/news/newsviews/newsviews031315.pdf

Running the Church is Not the Only Thing that Makes you Pope

If after all this, anyone still doubts that Benedict's renunciation was a qualified one, let us turn to the words he addressed to his old friend and fellow countryman, journalist and author Peter Seewald, in his 2016 book, *Last Testament: In His Own Words:*

Peter Seewald: "Is a slowdown in the ability to perform, reason enough to climb down from the chair of Peter?"

Pope Benedict: "One can of course make that accusation, but it would be a *functional misunderstanding. The follower of Peter is not merely bound to a function;* the office enters into your very being. In this regard, fulfilling a function is not the only criterion."[58]

Seewald merely repeated the words of Benedict's own *Declaratio* back to him and Benedict calls it an "accusation"? A "functional misunderstanding"?

---

[57] (footnote cont'd) Violi's position has evolved somewhat since. He now considers that Ratzinger did, in fact, renounce the office of Bishop of Rome, not simply its exercise: "The canonical *missio* entrusted to a bishop does not in fact entail the identification between the sacramental ontological *munus* and the office conferred upon him. If in the diocesan bishop *"munus"* and "office" coincide *manente officio*, at the moment of renunciation the episcopal see becomes vacant (Can. 416 CJC 1983). The renouncer loses his office and the powers attached to it. However, *the sacramental ontological participation of the renouncing bishop in the munera deriving from the [episcopal] consecration*, which do not involve the exercise of the powers attached to the office, does not disappear. The [Second Vatican] Council itself mentions, for example, a *sollicitudo* 'which, although not exercised by acts of jurisdiction, contributes greatly to the good of the universal Church' (LG 23)." Violi, *"Officium e munus tra ordinamento canonico e comunione ecclesiale,"* *Rivista telematica*, vol. 31 (2019), p. 140 ss; https://riviste.unimi.it/index.php/statoechiese/article/view/12353

[58] Peter Seewald, Benedict XVI, *Last Testament: In His Own Words*, (New York: Bloomsbury Continuum, 2016), Kindle Edition.

Yes. Anyone (Seewald included) who reads Benedict's *Declaratio* and concludes at face value that by giving up the "active" duties of a pope, Benedict ceased being papal, has not only misunderstood Benedict's intentions, but the Petrine ministry itself: "The follower of Peter [the Pope] is not merely bound to a function [i.e. active administration of the Roman see]... fulfilling a function is not the only criterion [for being Pope]":

> I had to...consider whether or not *functionalism would completely encroach on the papacy* ...Earlier, bishops were not allowed to resign...a number of bishops...said "I am a father and that I'll stay", because you can't simply stop being a father; *stopping is a functionalization and secularization, something from the sort of concept of public office that shouldn't apply to a bishop.* To that I must reply: even a father's *role* stops. Of course a father does not stop being a father, but he is relieved of *concrete responsibility. He remains a father in a deep, inward sense, in a particular relationship which has* **responsibility**, but *not with day-to-day tasks as such*...If he steps down, *he remains in an inner sense within the* **responsibility** *he took on*, but *not in the function*...one comes to understand that **the office of the Pope** *[Petrine munus] has lost none of its greatness*...[59]

In October 1977, during the symposium "On the Nature and Commission of the Petrine Ministry" marking the 80th birthday of Pope Paul VI (r. 1963-1978), Ratzinger declared:

> The "we" unity of Christians...is in turn maintained by *personal bearers of* **responsibility** for this unity, and it is once again *personified in* **Peter**—*in* **Peter**...through which demands are made of him as a person with *personal*

---

[59] Ibid.

*responsibility…this institution can exist only as a person and in particular and **personal responsibility**…*

He abides…*in **personal responsibility** for Christ; professing the Lord's death and Resurrection is his whole commission and **personal responsibility**…which forms the heart of the doctrine of papal primacy*, is therefore not opposed to the theology of the Cross…collegiality and primacy …do not merge in such a way that **the personal responsibility** ultimately disappears into anonymous governing bodies. Precisely in their inseparability, **personal responsibility** serves unity, which…bring about the more effectively, the more true it remains to its roots in the *theology of the Cross*.[60]

In 2016, Benedict says: "If he [the Pope] steps down, *he remains* in an inner sense *within the responsibility* he took on [the papacy], but *"not in the function,"* or "day-to-day tasks." In 1977, Ratzinger says: "**this institution [the papacy]** can_*exist only as a person* and in particular and **personal responsibility**…" He adds: "He abides in obedience and thus in **personal responsibility** for Christ; professing the Lord's death and Resurrection is *his whole commission and personal responsibility.*"

For Benedict, "personal responsibility" is the essence of what it means to be Pope. To be responsible not as a public official filled with day-to-day tasks, but *metaphysical* responsibility for the flock of Christ. In his Seewald interview, Benedict says that although he "stepped down," "HE REMAINS… within the *responsibility.*" Translation: *"He remains papal."* Thus, the "Pope" in "Pope Emeritus."

Benedict characterized Seewald's question as an accusation, as a *"functional* misunderstanding," as if Seewald had

---

[60] Cf. Nt. 53.

missed the transcendent component of the Petrine *munus* by suggesting: "whenever he is not *actively* leading the Church, he is not papal." Benedict corrects him by saying that the "office enters into your very being;" it is a sacramental, ontological "always."

Benedict once criticized Martin Luther precisely for misunderstanding the difference between office as jurisdiction or function and office as rite or sacrament:

> [For Luther] the priest does not transcend his role as preacher. The consequent restriction to the word alone had, as its logical outcome, the pure *functionality* of the priesthood: it consisted exclusively in a *particular activity; if that activity was missing, the ministry itself ceased to exist...* There was purposely no further mention of priesthood but only of "office;" the assignment of this office was, in itself, a secular act.[61]

Benedict made a similar observation regarding postconciliar conceptions of the Catholic priesthood:

> The crisis of the priesthood, which became obvious shortly after the Council...It resulted from a change in the meaning of life: the sacred was less understood while the *functional* was elevated to become the exclusively dominant category.

> Two conceptions of the priesthood were in confrontation: a *social functional* vision which defined the nature of the priesthood as a service to the community in the fulfillment of a *function* at the service of the social body of the Church. *The ontological-sacramental vision* which, while not denying the service character of the priesthood, *saw it anchored in the existence of the ministry, an existence that was determined by a*

---

[61] Joseph Ratzinger, *Principles of Catholic Theology*, p. 248.

gift, called a sacrament, and granted to him by the Lord through the Church. A shift of terminology accompanied the *functional* vision. One avoided using the words "priest" or "priestly" on account of the sacral meaning; in its place one used the neutral-*functional* term "minister" which at the moment had almost no importance in Catholic theology.[62]

Accordingly, in his 2013 *Declaratio*, Benedict renounced the functional ministry/service [*ministerium*] of the active Bishop of Rome, not the ontological "ministry [*munus*], an existence that was determined by a gift called a sacrament," or more simply put: the *Munus Petrinum*. As Cardinal Peter Erdö states: "as in the [Second Vatican] Council, even in the new Code [of Canon Law] '*munus*'...not infrequently also ...[has] a special, theological meaning of the three *munera* [ontological gifts][63] of Christ (can. 204 § 1)...see canon 375 § 2, 519). The passages in which the legislator speaks of the "*munus*" of Peter (can. 331) or the Roman Pontiff (can. 332 § 2, 333 §§ 1-2, 334) are connected with this sense."[64]

Ministerium means the same as *Munus*—Except When it Doesn't

This having been said, almost all readers of Benedict's *Declaratio*, specialist and non-specialist alike, have made the same "functional mistake" as Seewald, of *always* equating the terms *munus* and *ministerium*. They argue that by renouncing the *ministerium* of the Bishop of Rome, Benedict renounced the Petrine

---

[62] Joseph Ratzinger, "Life and Ministry of Priests," International Symposium on the Thirtieth Anniversary of the Promulgation of the Conciliar Decree *Presbyterorum Ordinis*, (23-28 October 1995); https://www.vatican.va/roman_curia/congregations/cclergy/documents/rc_con_cclergydoc24101995prh_en.html

[63] As Cardinal Raymond Burke says, "The *munus* is a grace that's conferred, and only in virtue of that grace can one carry out the ministry;" https://www.lifesitenews.com/news/did-benedict-really-resign-gaenswein-burke-and-brandmueller-weigh-in/

[64] Peter Erdö, "*Ministerium, munus* et *officium* in codice Iuris canonici," *Periodica de re morali canonica liturgica*, vol. 78, no. 4 (1989), pp. 411-436. Cf. Author's Preface, Nt. 1.

Munus or "Office" in its entirety. Typical is the argumentation of Fr. John Rickert, FSSP:

> In the first place, *ministerium* and *munus* are indeed synonymous, and the distinction attempted [by those claiming Benedict was still Pope] is not based on a correct interpretation of the words.

> *A Latin Dictionary* by Lewis and Short, which is a standard, well-respected dictionary of long standing, states simply that *ministerium* and *munus* are synonyms. See the entry for *munus*.
> But to indulge the proposed argument, we can look into this more diligently. Here is a remarkable resource for doing so: *A Guide to Dictionaries of Latin Synonyms...*

> 1. Robert Douthat, p. 96. "*Munus*" (*qua* debt or duty) "as a performance or function." (emphasis added) 2. Ferdinand Schultz (art. 280): "*Munus* (and in the plural, the seldom used *munia*) denotes the exercise of an obligation that is public and political" (emphasis added). Whereas *officium* arises more from the internal voice of conscience.[65]

But Bishop Juan Ignacio Arrieta, Secretary of the Pontifical Council for the Interpretation of Legislative Texts, however, teaches differently. He says that problems have arisen since the Council with regard to

> the public function and the notion of office [which] are particularly reflected in the *fluctuating* use of notions such as "*munus*", "*ministry*" and "*office*", both in doctrine and in the *official texts of the Church*...notions close to that of public

---

[65] John Rickert, FSSP, "*Munus, Ministerium* & Pope Emeritus Benedict;" https://www.wmbriggs.com/post/39718/

54

function, such as *"munus"*, "ministry" and "office"; terms which *do not find univocal content* in the documents of Vatican Council II, nor among the normative texts, being used indiscriminately by doctrine.[66]

Arrieta claims that *munus* and *ministerium* are *not synonymous* as used even in official documents. Anna Slowikowska, of the John Paul II Catholic University of Lublin in Poland, concurs:

The Latin noun munus is an ambiguous word. In the teaching of the Second Vatican Council this word is present up to 255 times, whereof 55 times in the Constitution *Lumen gentium.* The Council Fathers used this term in the meaning of: "office", "function", "mission", "service", "task", "obligation", "ministry". In many places the translations of the constitution from the Latin language into the Polish language in 1968 and 2002 are different. *This can cause not only problems of interpretation, but also doctrinal problems.*[67]

And Slowikowska refutes Rickert:

The knowledge of all the meanings of a given word — in this case munus — is not enough to correctly identify the thoughts of the author of the translated text.

The term *munus* is most often analyzed in the literature with two others: *officium* and *ministerium.* They are also synonymous with it. *But at the same time each of them can mean something different. Their use, whether separate or*

---

[66] Juan Ignacio Arrieta, "Funzione pubblica e ufficio ecclesiastico," *Ius Ecclesiae,* 7 (1995), pp. 92-93. My translation from the Italian.

[67] Anna Slowikowska, "Interpretacja pojęcia *munus* w Konstytucji dogmatycznej o Kościele *Lumen gentium,*" *Roczniki Humanistyczne,* LXIII, z8 (2015), pp. 125-145. My translation from the Polish.

synonymous, always depends on the context of the utterance, the author's intention, or the purpose for which they are used." [68]

Fortunately, in addition to Benedict's *Declaratio*, we do possess a document wherein he, himself, admits of a distinction between *munus* and *ministerium*: between the transcendent gift and the functional use of it. In the early 1980s, Ratzinger expresses his approval of the reform of the rite of ordination carried out in 1947:

> Pius XII defines as the central words those spoken at the consecration by the bishop: "Send forth upon him, O Lord, we beseech thee, the Holy Spirit, by whom may he (the ordained) be strengthened to perform faithfully the work of thy service with the help of thy sevenfold gift" *"Emitte in eum, quaesumus, Domine, Spiritum Sanctum, quo in opus* **ministerii** *tui fideliter exsequendi septiformis gratiae tuae* **munere** *roboretur."*

> Accordingly the key word now is *ministerium* or *munus*: service and gift." [69]

Ratzinger remarks that while the "medieval rite is formed on the pattern of investiture in a secular office. Its key word is *'potestas'* [power], the key words now are *"munus,"* the divine gift which allows *"ministerium,"* the service (active or passive) to God and His People.

A Sacramental Aspect to the Papacy?

Thus, we may conclude that for Ratzinger, the Pope may occupy an "office as jurisdiction," which comes and goes, but the

---

[68] Ibid.

[69] Ratzinger, *Principles of Catholic Theology*, p. 241.

interpenetrating spiritual "office as rite," being sacramental, is never lost. As de Mattei laments:

Vatican Council II did not explicitly reject the concept of *"potestas"* ["power"], but set it aside, replacing it with *an equivocal new concept, that of "munus."* Art. 21 of *"Lumen Gentium"* then seems to teach that episcopal consecration confers not only the fullness of orders, but also the *office* [*munera*] of teaching and governing, whereas in the whole history of the Church the act of episcopal consecration has been distinguished from that of appointment, or of the conferral of the canonical mission [by the Pope]. This *ambiguity* is consistent with the ecclesiology of the theologians of the Council and post-council (Congar, *Ratzinger*, de Lubac, Balthasar, Rahner, Schillebeeckx...) *who presumed to reduce the mission of the Church to a sacramental function, scaling down its juridical aspects...*

Ratzinger...distanced himself from tradition when he saw in the primacy of Peter the fullness of the apostolic ministry, **linking the ministerial character to the sacramental** [J. Auer-J. Ratzinger, *La Chiesa universale sacramento di salvezza*, Cittadella, Assisi, 1988].[70]

And to all of this, we must finally add the astute testimony of Carlo Fantappiè, Law Faculty of the University of Roma Tre. This is what he writes regarding Ratzinger's renunciation:

A third theological conception which, considering the articulation between person and office to be superseded, insists on *the sacramental foundation of the ministry and on the indelible bond of the sacrament with the mission. **Applied to the***

---

[70] de Mattei, "One and One Alone is Pope;" http://
chiesa.espresso.repubblica.it/articolo/1350868bdc4.html?eng=y

Petrine ministry, this doctrine postulates a distinction between munus and ministry and makes the primacy a sort of personal charism, giving rise to inconsistencies or misunderstandings, such as the *coexistence of two popes, even if one reigning and one emeritus...*

Against the prevailing juridical consideration of the canonists, who placed the power of jurisdiction at the center of the papal figure, as the origin of all the others in the Church, *the conciliar theologians have countered with the primariness of the sacramental dimension of the episcopate, from which derive the other specific functions of the bishop of Rome.*[71]

No less a person than Pope Francis, himself, confirms Fantappiè's observation: *"For some theologians the Papacy is a sacrament. The Germans are very creative in all these things. I do not think so, but I want to say that it is something special."*[72]

Fantappiè states further:

In my opinion, the interpretative question raised by Benedict XVI's announcement is to be traced back not so much to the distinction between *munus* and *executio* [Cf. Violi] or between the various papal *corpora*, as to the problem of *the relationship between the sacramental [sacred] and ministerial [functional] dimensions.* One would refer to the ontological structure, the other to historical implementation. In this case the *munus petrinum*, although not a grade of Order, would refer to *a permanent mission of a sacramental nature which would not cease with the loss of the office-ministry."*

[71] Carlo Fantappiè, *Ecclesiologia e Canonistica*, (Venezia: Marcianum Press, 2015), p. 391. My translation from the Italian.

[72]http://www.archivioradiovaticana.va/storico/2015/03/13/pope_francis_on_his_pontificate_to_date/en-1129074

...starting from the principle of the divine elevation of the pope, from the absolutist conception of his power and from the *special sacramental bond that the elect contracts at the moment of election,* succeeds in affirming the ontological character of the bond between the person and the office ending up by considering *the resignation of the pontificate theologically impossible.*[73]

Fantappiè's explanation is especially prescient because he maintains that the *"special sacramental bond"* of the person elected Pope *"contracts at the moment of election."* In other words, the Petrine *munus* although *"sacramental"* [office as rite] is NOT the same sacramental *munus* received at episcopal consecration.[74] And this is in direct opposition to Geraldina Boni, Faculty of Law of the University of Bologna, who holds: "Ratzinger still exercises, to the benefit of the Church, a very high spiritual ministry: but bound not to the *munus* (*officium*) of which he was invested with the legitimate election, accepted by him, as pontiff, but to the sacramental *munus* transmitted to him with the episcopal ordination."[75]

Fantappiè's book first appeared in 2015, but in May of 2016, his view of Ratzinger's renunciation was confirmed by none other than Georg Gänswein, in his speech at the Gregorianum:

The key word in that statement [Benedict's *Declaratio*] is *munus Petrinum,* translated —as happens most of the time — with "Petrine ministry." And yet, *munus,* in Latin, has a multiplicity of meanings: it can mean service, duty, guide or *gift,* even prodigy. *Before and after his resignation,* Benedict *understood and understands his task as participation in such a*

---

[73] Fantappiè, p. 393.

[74] Cf. Appendix I.

[75] Geraldina Boni, *Sopra una Rinuncia,* (Bologna: Bononia University Press, 2015), p. 196. My translation from the Italian.

"Petrine ministry" [His Petrine *munus*—not his episcopal *munus*]. He has left the papal throne [office as jurisdiction] and yet, with the step made on February 11, 2013, he has not at all abandoned this ministry [*munus*/office as rite]. Instead, he has complemented the personal office *with a collegial and synodal dimension, as a quasi-shared ministry* (*als einen quasi gemeinsamen Dienst*)...

...he has not abandoned the Office of Peter—something which would have been entirely impossible for him after his irrevocable acceptance of the office in April 2005. By an act of extraordinary courage, he has instead renewed this office (even against the opinion of well-meaning and undoubtedly competent advisers), and with a final effort he has strengthened it (as I hope)...To date, in fact, *there has never been a step like that taken by Benedict XVI.* So it is not surprising that it has been seen by some as revolutionary...

"He has not abandoned the Office of Peter," is a most troubling statement. According to Canon Law, Can. 332 § 2: "If it happens that the Roman Pontiff *resigns his office,* it is required for validity that the resignation is made freely and properly manifested..."

To validly resign, a pope *must abandon* the Office of Peter/Petrine *Munus.*

Now Boni and other scholars are nearly unanimous in their belief that by renouncing the office of jurisdiction, i.e. "the active ministry," Benedict, in fact, complied with Canon 232 § 2 and has, therefore, validly resigned:

The loss, then, of the office [as jurisdiction] with renunciation does not eliminate the *munus* or *ministerium* as we have understood them, as an 'ontological qualification' [office as rite]: thus the bishop emeritus, as specified in the already mentioned document of the Congregation for Bishops of 2008, retains forever, and continues to exercise, but in a particular way, the function of teaching, sanctifying and governing...All this is also valid for the pope, bishop of Rome, *mutatis mutandis* with regard to the office held: the pontiff who has renounced conserves the *munus* received with the episcopal consecration which cannot be nullified and annihilated, as has already been argued at length. He can renounce the "office" of pope: for this reason the word *officium* should perhaps have appeared in canon 332 § 2, and in any case this is how it is rendered in the various national languages; and in fact, the diocesan bishop is invited by canon 401 to renounce the *officium*...Evidently, therefore, in canon 332 § 2, in that "*muneri suo renuntiet*"—where *muneri suo renuntiet* implies ownership of the office—, *munus* is used (with a certain degree of "approximation") not in a "sacramental" sense, but in a "juridical" sense.[76]

But Benedict, as we have seen, traced the origin of his ontological "office of rite," not to his episcopal ordination in May 1977, but to his election as Pope in April 2005. Both he and Gänswein reaffirmed multiple times (by various turns of phrase) that he did not abandon the Office of Peter—at least not in a metaphysical sense. They both declare that *he was a current Successor of St. Peter—not a former one*: Benedict: "The *follower of Peter* is not merely bound to a function [administering Rome and the Church universal];" Gänswein: "today we live with *two living successors of Peter* among us..."

Thus, we have a *Catch-22* situation. The law as written says that if the Pope wishes to step down, he must renounce his

---

[76] Geraldina Boni, *Sopra una Rinuncia*, pp. 179-181.

[Petrine] *munus*, that is, release *what* he had hitherto been bound to beginning at his elevation. But if he wills to return only the functional *munus*, while willing to keep the spiritual *munus*, has he really complied with the law? (And if there is no spiritual *papal munus*, then he was in serious error.) Can one accurately assert that one's renunciation was valid, if one professes with equal enthusiasm that he is still a "follower of Peter," that, in fact, "the office" entered "into his very being"? Can he really "remain in an inner sense within the responsibility [papacy] he took on, but not in the function [bishop of Rome]"?[77]

There are those who argue that because Benedict renounced the "ministry of Bishop of Rome," because he stated that "the Chair would be vacant," and that "a successor" would necessarily need to be elected, therefore, his renunciation was valid. But giving up active service, allowing someone else to serve in that capacity is not the same as renouncing one's ontological status as Vicar of Christ. Let us take the example of Blessed Karl I, Emperor of Austria-Hungary.

On the losing side of World War I, in November 1918, Karl was forced to relinquish his power, but this was not the same thing as "abdicating" as God's monarch. As Suzanne Pearson explains:

---

[77] "The pope must entirely renounce his papal *munus* without retaining anything of it in order to cease to hold office as pope, because unlike a bishop, who does not need to entirely renounce his episcopal *munus*, but only his *munus* as diocesan ordinary — intending not to cease being a bishop, but only to cease being the ordinary over his diocese — the pope, in order to relinquish the papacy, must not merely intend to relinquish his power of ordinary jurisdiction over the universal Church, but he must intend altogether to cease being the pope in order to relinquish his office. The reason for this is that a Bishop Emeritus is still a bishop, but a retired bishop, but a pope who renounces his *munus* ceases to be pope, and as a former pope, he is only a retired bishop. Accordingly, a pope must renounce entirely the Petrine *munus* in order to cease to be pope, and if he expresses an intention to retain anything whatever of the papal *munus* in his act of renunciation, the act is null and void." Fr. Paul Kramer, *On the True and False Pope: The Case Against Bergoglio, To Deceive the Elect* Vol. II, (Gondolin Press, 2021) Kindle Edition.

for several generations, English speaking authors write that he abdicated, although it is easily proven that he did not. If he had abdicated after the War, why did they keep pressuring him during exile to abdicate? If he had abdicated at any time during his Swiss exile, why did they send a special delegation to get him to abdicate after his second restoration trip to Hungary? When he again refused, he was "dethroned"...sent as a prisoner to the island of Madeira.[78]

Let us turn then to an examination of his Declaration:

Ever since my accession I have tried ceaselessly to lead my peoples out of the horrors of a war for whose inception I bear no trace of blame.

I have not hesitated to restore constitutional life and I have opened up for the peoples the path of their development as independent states.

Filled, now as ever, with unwavering devotion to all my peoples, I do not wish to oppose their free growth with my own person.

I recognize in advance whatever decision that German-Austria may make about its future political form.

The people, through its representatives, has taken over the government. **I renounce all [active] participation in the affairs of state.**

At the same time, I relieve my Austrian Government from office.

May the people of German-Austria, in unity and tolerance create and strengthen the new order! The happiness of my peoples has, from the beginning, been the object of my most ardent wishes.

Only an inner peace can heal the wounds of this war.

---

[78] Suzanne Pearson, personal email to this author.

No. He very carefully did not abdicate, but in his statement (reproduced above) chose words that left open the possibility of a legal return to rule: *"Ich verzichte auf jeden Anteil an den Staatsgeschäften"*. A translation follows; then the document rearranged so as to be readable. The second signature is Professor Lammasch, the Prime Minister.[79]

As William O'Reilly, Professor at Cambridge University confirms: "The oath as king of Hungary was for life and indissoluble; *a king could not divorce his crown, his land, his people.* No Hungarian king has abdicated."[80]

"A Resignation Made Out of...Substantial Error...is Invalid By the Law Itself"

If Ratzinger resigned believing he could remain "pope" sacramentally, even after relinquishing the "active" exercise of the Bishop of Rome, what are the consequences if he was objectively wrong?

What if the new bishop of Rome in accepting his election *merely receives an office of jurisdiction* "neatly separated" from his pre-existing episcopal ministry [sacramental episcopal *munus*] as was the Church's understanding for hundreds of years? As Robert Siscoe writes:

> *What makes a man Pope is possessing the jurisdiction of the papal office.* Jurisdiction is what gives the Pope the authority to "actively exercise the ministerium," by teaching, governing and sanctifying. Jurisdiction is the *form* of the Papal office.[81]

[79] https://www.austrianphilately.com/ausintrans/karl.htm

[80] William O'Reilly, personal email to this author.

[81] http://www.trueorfalsepope.com/p/the-validity-of-benedicts-resignation.html;

If this is true, then the object Ratzinger renounced—the "ministry of the Bishop of Rome"—was erroneously understood, a circumstance known as "substantial error." And as Canon 188 of the Church's Code of Canon Law states: "A resignation made out of grave fear that is inflicted unjustly or out of malice, *substantial error*, or simony *is invalid by the law itself.*"

Under this scenario, Benedict, believing he was retaining the Petrine "office as rite" while relinquishing the "office as jurisdiction" would have been operating under a false base premise. Therefore, his resignation would be invalid, and he would remain the lawful pope (making Francis an antipope).[82]

Some have objected that if Benedict had believed the papacy to be sacramental, he would have been a *heretic* and, therefore, incapable of being a valid pope in the first place.[83] But his error (assuming it is an error) does not rise to the level of heresy. True, Vatican II declared episcopal power, not papal power, the fullness of Holy Orders, that bishops have a sacramental *munus* (it said nothing about the Pope). But this novel teaching *is not dogmatic*; its modification is not heresy—Benedict, himself, admits as much.[84]

---

[82] Cf. also Can. 126: "An act placed out of ignorance or *out of error concerning something which constitutes its substance or which amounts to a condition sine qua non is invalid.*"

[83] Cf. Steven O'Reilly, *Valid? The Resignation of Benedict XVI* (Atlanta, GA: Hartwell) Kindle Edition. Cf. also de Mattei: "If...Benedict XVI had the intention of dividing it [the papacy], of modifying the constitution of the Church willed by Our Lord, he would have fallen into heresy, with all the problems that would ensue;" https://www.lifesitenews.com/news/did-benedict-really-resign-gaenswein-burke-and-brandmueller-weigh-in/

[84] Cf. Appendix I, esp. p.95; Ratzinger affirms "the sacramentality of the episcopal office 'most nearly approaches being a dogma,' because of the solemnity of the introductory words 'This sacred Council teaches,' but even it should not be considered a dogma, for the text does not state that this doctrine is part of the apostolic deposit of faith, *nor that it be received with the assent of faith;*" ...

Still others have objected that if Ratzinger had, not an heretical, but just simply an erroneous understanding of the papacy—enough to invalidate his renunciation—then by the same reasoning, it would have invalidated his initial acceptance of the Petrine Office. But Benedict's novel view, that office of jurisdiction and office of rite combine, only causes difficulty when one tries to separate the two.

A closer look at the impediment of substantial error confirms this. John Beal, Professor of Canon Law of the Catholic University of America writes: "Substantial error is a mistaken judgment which affects the essential elements of resignation... *either the cause or motivation for resignation or the nature of resignation and its consequences.*"[85] Or as William Cahill, of St. John's University explains:

> error invalidates the act if it is an error concerning the substance of the act...Error affects consent, for the will in an act of consent elects an object presented to it by the mind. *If the mind is in error, the object is imperfectly or incorrectly presented,* and choice made upon such a premise is not always the same choice that would have been made if the object were correctly known.[86]

A practical example may help illustrate the concept. Let us suppose my eccentric old grandmother has left me her estate. Among her items I find a statue of an elephant, a rather big,

---

84 (footnote cont'd) Joseph Ratzinger, "La collégialité épiscopale, développement théologique," Translation into French by R. Virrion, in *L'Église de Vatican II: Études autour de la Constitution conciliare sur l'Église,* vol. 2, ed. Guilherme Baraúna, French edition ed. Yves M-J. Congar (Paris: Cerf, 1966), pp. 763-90; 789. Translation and citation, Lawrence King, *The Authoritative Weight of Non-Definitive Magisterial Teaching,* (2016), p. 129.

85 John P. Beal et al., eds., *New Commentary on the Code of Canon Law,* (New York, NY: Paulist Press, 2000), p. 221-222.

86 William F Cahill, "Fraud and Error in the Canon Law of Marriage," *The Catholic Lawyer* (April 1955), vol. 1, no. 2.

gawdy, gleaming gold elephant that weighs a ton. The statue not being to my liking, I decide to sell it at a garage sale. Believing it to be gold-plated I do not sell it too cheaply, but neither do I ask for a fortune for it either.

But what if, in fact, the rather big, gawdy, gleaming gold elephant that weighs a ton—was actually made out of solid gold? In parting with it, I have committed (quite a) substantial error! (And lost hundreds of thousands of dollars to boot!) In fact, my will was not free in this alleged free market transaction because I lacked truly <u>informed consent</u>. My intellect had an erroneous appraisal of the object that I was relinquishing to another. I misunderstood its proper nature.[87]

If Benedict misunderstood the very thing he was renouncing, thinking he could remain a (passive) successor of Peter after leaving active service, when no such thing is possible, then not simply according to canon law, but according to Natural Law his act was not free and, therefore, was invalid.

It is as if he said, "I will only resign the active administration of Rome and the Universal Church, if I can remain a passive or spiritual successor of Peter [Pope Emeritus]." This is like a man saying, "I will only marry a Russian Imperial Romanov," who then marries Natasha Romanova from Marvel Comics' Avengers. He has committed substantial error because he is wrong about the essence of who she is—she is not an actual daughter or granddaughter of the last Tsar, Nicholas II.

---

[87] "The error is substantial when it falls on the nature of the contract, on the object of the contract, or on the quality of the object that can be considered substantial. Properties are considered substantial when the object, without them, would fall into a different category of things, as it would be if a gilded chain were sold for a gold chain." Fr. Franz Xavier Wernz, SJ, Fr. Pedro Vidal, SJ, *Ius Canonicum*, II, (1943), pp. 49-50.

In fact, substantial error is something which does arise in marriage cases. This is important because many critics of the "Benedict-Is-Pope hypothesis" cite Ratzinger's own testimony that his will was free and so his renunciation must have been valid. In response to veteran Vatican journalist, Andrea Tornielli, Benedict allegedly quipped: "There is absolutely no doubt regarding the validity of my resignation from the Petrine ministry...The only condition for the validity of my resignation is the complete freedom of my decision. Speculations regarding its validity are simply absurd."[88] But many couples throughout the world will likewise swear up and down that their marriage is valid, whereas, in fact, according to Natural Law and the laws of the Church, at least some of these marriages are not.

In this precise regard, another objection that has been raised is that we cannot read Ratzinger's mind. The whole notion of his resignation being invalid due to his erroneous understanding is illusory since "the Church does not judge the internal forum." The answer to this objection is: Yes and No.

Yes, the pope might have resigned out of pride, for example, or embarrassment, or despair—or because he wanted to spend more time with his cat! These are his personal intentions to which the rest of humanity have no access. But this is not the intention which we are speaking about.

We are *not* speaking about "the *finis cujus gratia opus fit*, the end for which one does something, which is *extrinsic* to it." We are speaking about the very

---

[88] Andrea Tornielli, "Ratzinger: 'My resignation is valid. Speculations are simply absurd'," *La Stampa*, (February 28, 2014); https://www.lastampa.it/vatican-insider/en/2014/02/28/news/ratzinger-my-resignation-is-valid-speculations-are-simply-absurd-1.35928994

finis operis, the intrinsic end of the work itself. Personal motivations (the subjective intention) could be very difficult to determine, and are often a combination of many different reasons…[but] for whatever personal reasons, the person wants to do *something*…[89]

A famous example from history should suffice to explain. In 1896, in the document *Apostolicae Curae*, Pope Leo XIII declared all Anglican orders invalid. What is key for us, is that the Pope attributed this partly due to *defect of intention* even though intention is normally part of the internal forum:

> [D]efect of "intention"…is equally essential to the Sacrament. The Church does not judge about the mind and intention, in so far as it is something by its nature internal; but *in so far as it is manifested externally, she is bound to judge concerning it.* A person who has…used the requisite matter and form to effect and confer a sacrament is presumed for that very reason to have intended to do (*intendisse*) what the Church does…On the other hand, *if the rite be changed, with the manifest intention of introducing another rite not approved by the Church and of rejecting what the Church does, and what, by the institution of Christ, belongs to the nature of the Sacrament,* then …not only is the *necessary intention wanting* to the Sacrament, but that the *intention is adverse to and destructive of* the Sacrament.[90]

So it *is* possible to judge Benedict's objective intention (not his personal motivation) from an examination of the words he used in his *Declaratio*. True, resignation is not a sacramental act, nevertheless, if Benedict deviated from the traditional expression

---

[89] Rev. Damien Dutertre, "On the Lack of Intention to Accept the Papacy;" https://mostholytrinityseminary.org/wpcontent/uploads/2022/06/Lack_of_Intention_Dutertre_2022.pdf

[90] Pope Leo XIII, *Apostolicae Curae*, 1896, 33.

of resignation (i.e. "if the rite is changed") and if his words (and actions) contradict what "belongs to the nature" of resignation and/or "the nature" of the Papacy, one *can* judge it to be invalid. His renunciation was, after all, a legal act:

> By legal transaction is ordinarily understood a juridical act...a direct manifestation of intention or will to produce a juridical effect. Hence, the essential requisites of every legal transaction are: (a) *will or intention of the subject*...(b) their competence (natural or legal)...(c) *external manifestation*, without which the internal will has no legal force or value...just as if you ate meat on Friday thinking it was a Thursday, you did not sin...you did not intend to...eat meat on Friday, so also, *whenever the internal intention does not correspond to the legal transaction posited.*
>
> What matters is therefore the objective intention, manifested externally, which is necessarily included in the subjective intention, which is internal...[not] the personal, subjective, intention motivating someone to do something, which would answer the question:...Why do you want to do this thing? It is sufficient to observe that, whatever his personal motives are, the person in fact *clearly manifests the intention to do something.* [91]

Benedict, in his *Declaratio*, manifested his intention externally when he explicitly said: "I am well aware that this *munus* [office], due to its *essential spiritual nature*, must be carried out not only with words and deeds, but *no less with prayer and suffering;*" he *will continue* the prayer and suffering, therefore, he will *continue* participating in the *Petrine munus*. And Can. 331 specifically states that a pope's power comes from

---

[91] Pio Ciprotti, article "Act, Juridical," in the *Dictionary of Moral Theology,* Roberti and Palazzini, (Westminster MD, 1962); As cited in Dutertre, "On the Lack of Intention."

making the *munus* his own: "The bishop of the Roman Church, in whom continues the *munus* given by the Lord uniquely to Peter… and to be transmitted to his successors…By virtue of <u>his</u> *munus*, he possesses supreme, full, immediate, and universal ordinary power…"

Benedict never renounced the *munus* and so he implicitly attempted to share it with the new Bishop of Rome. This amounts to a bifurcation of the papacy, which is not canonically or metaphysically possible.[92]

---

[92] Paul Kramer, *To Deceive the Elect*, "A partial act of renunciation is null and void due to *defect of* intention, 'To the Pontiff, as one (person) and alone, it was given to be the head;'" Domenico Gravina, OP, 1610.

Chapter Three
The Third Secret:
Satanic Apostasy "From the Top"

"The [papal] election of a heretic, schismatic, or female would be
null and void." [93]
The Catholic Encyclopedia, 1911

"Satan Must Reign in the Vatican. The Pope Will Be His Slave."
Roman Freemasonic Banner, 1917

"In an extreme case, a pope could become a heretic as a private
person and thus *automatically* lose his office if the contradiction to
the revelation and the dogmatic teaching of the church is
evident." [94]
Cardinal Gerhard Müller, 2022

"We are witnessing a process – apparently irreversible – of
apostasy of the Faith; a process which is the opposite of what St.
Leo the Great described in celebrating the solemnity of the Holy
Apostles Peter and Paul, in which he praised the providential role
of the *Alma Urbe,* the beloved City of Rome: having been a teacher
of error, Rome became a disciple of the Truth, wrote the great
Pontiff. Today we could say, with the dismay of children betrayed
by their father, that the Rome of the Martyrs and Saints having
been a teacher of Truth, has become a disciple of error. Because the
present apostasy, which involves civil and religious authority in a
rebellion against God the Creator and Redeemer, did not start
from below, but *from the top.*"
Archbishop Carlo Maria Vigano, 2022

---

[93] W. Fanning, "Papal Elections," *The Catholic Encyclopedia,* (New York, NY:
Robert Appleton Company, 1911); http://www.newadvent.org/cathen/11456a.htm
[94] Cardinal Gerhard Müller, (November 18, 2022); https://www.kath.net/
news/80010

In 1941, Sister Lucia did not flinch to record the ominous words of the "Second Secret" of Fatima, namely, that Russia "will spread her errors throughout the world, *causing wars and persecutions* of the Church. The good will be martyred, the Holy Father will have much to suffer, *various nations will be annihilated.*" But when instructed by her superiors to reveal the "Third Secret of Fatima," Lucia experienced the most mystifying hesitation:

> Having received the formal order to write down the Secret in mid-October [1943], two months later Sister Lucy still had not done so...Indeed as she took up her pen, she found herself incapable of writing. For, as she added in her letter to Don Garcia asking for his advice, *she had wanted to obey several times, and she had sat down to write, without being able to.* This mysterious impediment still existed on December 24, 1943, where she makes it clear in a letter to Don Garcia *"that this phenomenon was not due to natural causes."*

> ...On January 9, 1944, she wrote to Bishop da Silva:
> «I have written what you asked me; God willed to try me a little, but finally, this was indeed His will: (the text) is sealed in an envelope and the latter is in the notebooks...»[95]

> ...Canon Martins dos Reis...informs us of an immensely significant event: it was the Virgin Mary Herself who came in an apparition, to finally dispel the seer's darkness and put an end to her painful trial. Our author writes:

---

[95] Alonso, *Fatima 50*, p. 11; as cited in Frère Michel of the Holy Trinity, *The Whole Truth About Fatima, Vol. III: The Secret and the Church*, (Buffalo, NY: Immaculate Heart Publications, 1990), pp. 46-47.

«Before this apparition of the Mother of God, at the infirmary of Tuy, three times the seer had attempted to write the Secret in order to obey the order of Don José Alves Correia da Silva, but she was never capable. Only after this vision was she able to do so without the slightest difficulty, and at the same time was liberated from the great perplexity she found herself in, due to the different attitudes of the two prelates (Bishop da Silva and Archbishop Garcia y Garcia.»[96]

What could possibly be contained in the Secret that is so terrible that it took supernatural intervention for Lucia to confide it to paper?

What we do know is that as early as 1952, the Vatican sent a representative to Lucia to learn its explosive contents:

In a letter to the [Second Vatican] Council Fathers [in 1963], Father Schweigl writes that on March 27, 1952 he had received permission from the Pope to speak with Sister Lucia «about 31 questions concerning the conversion of Russia». On September 2, 1952 he had conversed with Sister Lucia about Messages of Our Lady of Fatima.[97]

Although the Holy Office did not authorize the publication of this interrogation, on his return to the Russicum Father Schweigl confided this to one of his colleagues who questioned him on the Secret: "I cannot reveal anything of what I learned at Fatima concerning the third Secret, but I can say that it has two parts: *one concerns the Pope*. The other, logically — although I must say nothing — would

---

[96] Martins dos Reis, *O Milagre do Sol e o Segredo do Fatima*, p. 121; as cited Ibid.

[97] http://www.1260.org/Mary/Apparitions_Fatima/Fatima_3rd_Secret_Two_Parts_Schweigl_en.htm

have to be the continuation of the words: *In Portugal the dogma of the Faith will always be preserved.*"[98]

St. Padre Pio and Exorcist Fr. Amorth

So something about the Pope and about the preservation of the Faith (or lack thereof) is apparently in the Third Secret. Do we have additional testimony? It seems we do, and from one of the greatest saints of the 20th century, St. Pio of Pietrelcina (d. 1968)! According to Fr. Gabriele Amorth (d. 2016), the late Chief Exorcist of the Diocese of Rome,

> Fr. Amorth: "One day Padre Pio said to me very sorrowfully: 'You know, Gabriele? *It is Satan who has been introduced into the bosom of the Church and within a very short time will come to rule a false Church.*'"

> Zavala: "Oh my God! Some kind of Antichrist! When did he prophesy this to you?"

> Fr. Amorth: "*It must have been about 1960*, since I was already a priest then."

> Zavala: "*Was that why John XXIII had such a panic about publishing the Third Secret of Fatima, so that the people wouldn't think that he was the anti-pope or whatever it was …?*"

> A slight but knowing smile curls the lips of Father Amorth.

> Zavala: "Did Padre Pio say anything else to you about future catastrophes: earthquakes, floods, wars, epidemics,

---

[98] Letter to Frère Michel, *The Whole Truth*, p. 710. Only words of Our Lady to Lucia on the Secret revealed.

76

hunger…? Did he allude to the same plagues prophesied in the Holy Scriptures?"

Fr. Amorth: "Nothing of the sort mattered to him, however terrifying they proved to be, except for *the great apostasy within the Church.* This was the issue that really tormented him and for which he prayed and offered a great part of his suffering, crucified out of love."

Zavala: *"The Third Secret of Fatima?"*

Fr. Amorth: "Exactly."

Zavala: "Is there any way to avoid something so terrible, Fr. Gabriele?"

Fr. Amorth: "There is hope, but it's useless if it's not accompanied by works. Let us begin by consecrating Russia to the Immaculate Heart of Mary, let us recite the Holy Rosary, let us all do prayer and penance…"[99]

Some would object that this is third-party testimony, i.e. Zavala quoting Amorth, quoting Padre Pio. But what is reported by Zavala is consistent with what Amorth said, for example, in 2010: "The Devil resides in the Vatican and you can see the consequences."[100]

---

[99] José María Zavala, *El Sécreto Mejor Guardado de Fátima,* (Madrid: Planeta Publishing, 2017); as cited in Maike Hickson, "Chief Exorcist Father Amorth: Padre Pio Knew The Third Secret," *One Peter Five* (May 23, 2017); https://onepeterfive.com/chief-exorcist-father-amorth-padre-pio-knew-the-third-secret/; Zavala claims to have interviewed Fr. Amorth in 2011.

[100] Nick Squires, "Chief exorcist says Devil is in Vatican," *The Telegraph* (March 11, 2010); https://www.telegraph.co.uk/news/worldnews/europe/vaticancityandholysee/7416458

So the Third Secret seemingly speaks of *"Satan... introduced into the bosom of the Church...come to rule a false Church...[an] anti-pope or whatever..."* Now *that* would explain why Sr. Lucia could not bring herself to pen such words![101]

But has anyone else privy to the Third Secret ever corroborated such chilling content?

From the Top

As we mentioned in the Introduction above, in *The Keys of This Blood*, Malachi Martin wrote that:

three dreadful outcomes are possible. Any of them could—probably would—entail the final disintegration of this Roman Catholic institutional organization...

The first possible outcome is the day when: "a sizable body of...clergy and laity, become convinced—rightly or wrongly—that *the then occupant of the apostolic throne of Peter is not, perhaps never was, a validly elected pope."*[102]

One year later, Martin let slip to an audience in Detroit, Michigan: "We're facing...what we may have to face, *finally...the False Pope."*[103]

During the 1990s, Martin was a repeated guest on the "Coast to Coast" late night show of radio personality, Art Bell. In a show with Martin broadcast live on July 13, 1998,[104] Bell read a

---

[101] An antipope and a false Church, the subjects, respectively, of Volumes One and Two of this present series on the Third Secret of Fatima and the Synodal Church.

[102] https://www.youtube.com/watch?v=3Qf7khkDXSI

[103] Martin, *Keys*, p. 677.

[104] The 91st anniversary of the Virgin of Fatima first revealing the Secret; https://www.youtube.com/watch?v=YCzryXT_whk&t=6833s

message from a listener in Australia: "I had a Jesuit priest tell me more of the Third Secret of Fatima years ago in Perth. He said, among other things, *the last pope would be under the control of Satan.* Pope John [XXIII] fainted thinking it might be him. We were interrupted before I could hear the rest."

Martin remarked, almost matter-of-factly: *"It sounds as if they were reading or...being told the text of the third secret; sounds like it, but it's sufficiently vague to make one hesitate; sounds like it."*[105]

Only "sounds like it"? "Sufficiently vague to make one hesitate"? Did Martin say this because the caller said "pope" and not "antipope"? Fr. Paul Kramer once told Martin he had deduced that the Secret referenced an antipope who is a heretic, and he replied, "Were it only that!"[106]

Twice now, we have seen the name of Pope John XXIII in connection with the Third Secret of Fatima, first with Zavala and again with the Australian caller. This is because Our Lady said that the Secret was to be revealed by 1960 "at the latest" and Pope John (r. 1958-1963) made the fatal decision not to reveal it. Why did he choose not to obey Our Lady? Pope John's personal secretary, Monsignor Capovilla, was asked by the official archivist of Fatima, Fr. Alonso, in 1978.

Fr. Alonso asked: "Some reasons perhaps were: a) because it names expressly certain nations or hierarchs of the Church (cardinals, bishops)? ; b) because there were references to the religious crisis in the Church? ; c) because there were references—yet again—to Russia and its influence on the world?"[107]

---

[105] Ibid.

[106] https://rumble.com/v1d7wut-tce-46-fr.-paul-kramer-and-fatima.html

[107] *Rosarium*, 4-5 a. XI, (1978) as cited in Antonio Socci, *The Fourth Secret of Fatima*, (Loretto Publications, 2009), p. 150.

Capovilla responded: "It does not appear to me that what is involved is a motive to keep in reserve the names of persons and nations, or, of references of a political nature."[108] In other words, not possibilities "a" or "c," but "b"—"references to the religious crisis in the Church."

In similar fashion, Cardinal Ciappi, another Third Secret reader and personal papal theologian to Popes John XXIII, Paul VI, and John Paul II, wrote in a letter to a Professor Baumgartner of Salzburg: "In the Third Secret it is foretold, among other things, that the great apostasy in the Church *will begin at the top.*"[109]

As any Catholic (or non-Catholic) knows, the top of the Catholic Church is the papacy itself.

Fr. Alonso concludes of the Third Secret:

It is therefore completely probable that the text makes concrete references to the crisis of faith within the Church and to the negligence of the pastors themselves [and the] *internal struggles in the very bosom of the Church* and of *grave pastoral negligence of the upper hierarchy ...*

In the period preceding the great triumph of the Immaculate Heart of Mary, terrible things are to happen. These form the content of the third part of the Secret. What are they? If "in Portugal the dogma of the Faith will always be preserved,"...it can be clearly deduced from this that in other parts of the Church these dogmas are going to become obscure or even lost altogether...

[108] Ibid.

[109] Fr. Gerard Mura, "The Third Secret of Fatima: Has It Been Completely Revealed?," *Catholic* (March 2002); as cited https://fatima.org/some-other-witnesses-1930s-2003/

Does the unpublished text speak of concrete circumstances? It is very possible that it speaks not only of a real crisis of the faith in the Church during this in-between period, but like the secret of La Salette, for example, there are more concrete references to the internal struggles of Catholics or to the fall of priests and religious. *Perhaps it even refers to the failures of the upper hierarchy of the Church.* For that matter, none of this is foreign to other communications Sister Lucia has had on this subject.

An inopportune revelation of the text would only have further exasperated the two tendencies which continue to tear the Church apart: a traditionalism which would believe itself to be assisted by the Fatima prophecies, and a progressivism which would have lashed out against these apparitions, which in such a scandalous manner would seem to put the brakes on the conciliar Church's forward progress...Pope Paul VI judged it opportune and prudent to delay the revelation of the text until better times. Pope John XXIII declared that the text did not refer to his pontificate...And the following popes did not consider that the moment had come to lift the veil of mystery, in circumstances where the Church has still not overcome the frightening impact of twenty post-conciliar years, during which the crisis of the Faith has installed itself *at every level.*[110]

Dr. Alice Von Hildebrand testified that her famous philosopher-husband Dietrich, met in June of 1965 with Msgr. Mario Boehm, one of the editors of *L'Osservatore Romano*:

---

[110] Fr. Joaquin Alonso; *La Verdad sobre el Secreto de Fatima* (1976); Cf. Frère Michel, *The Whole Truth*, Vol. III, p. 687, pp.704-705; Cf. also *De nuevo el Secreto de Fatima* (1982) *Ephemerides mariologicae*, p. 93.

My husband raised the question: "Why was the third secret of Fatima not revealed?" For the Holy Virgin had said it should be shared with the faithful in 1960.

Don Mario: It was not revealed because of its content.

My husband: What was so fearful about it?

Msgr. Boehm (as a well-trained Italian) did not say that he had read it, but intimated that the content was fearful: *"infiltration of the Church to the very top"*.[111]

Then there is the testimony of Archbishop Marcel Lefebvre, founder of the Society of St. Pius X:

…there are apparitions…and these apparitions have been recognized by the See of Peter, *Fatima, La Salette, that say that the devil will climb to the highest places in the Church*, *I don't know if by the "highest place in the Church" that means Secretary of State, and then stops there, or if it goes even farther, if it goes all the way to the Pope. I don't know maybe even to someone who says he's the Pope*, I don't know, but you know this is something that isn't impossible and theologians have studied this problem, the theologians have studied this problem to see if it's something that can happen, *if a Pope can perhaps be a heretic and as a result excommunicated from the Church and therefore all his acts become illegitimate and invalid*.[112]

---

[111] Fr. Brian Harrison, Dr. Alice von Hildebrand, "Alice Von Hildebrand Sheds New Light on Fatima," *One Peter Five* (May 12, 2016); https://onepeterfive.com/alice-von-hildebrand-sheds-new-light-fatima

[112] Archbishop Marcel Lefebvre; http://www.archbishoplefebvre.com/blog/category/the%20church

Third Secret Finally Revealed?

After decades of criticism for its silence, in a dramatic move in June of 2000, the Vatican officially released a "vision" purportedly written by Sr. Lucia and constituting the "text" of the Third Secret.[113] The Vatican provided a view of the Secret by Cardinals Bertone (and Sodano) and a theological commentary of this view by Joseph Ratzinger—who publicly contradicted his previous statement (to Vittorio Messori in his 1984 interview) about the Secret and the "*Novissimi*"—when he declared:

> First of all we must affirm with Cardinal Sodano: "...the events to which the third part of the 'secret' of Fatima refers now seem part of the past". Insofar as individual events are described, they belong to the past. *Those who expected exciting apocalyptic revelations about the end of the world or the future course of history are bound to be disappointed.*[114]

Indeed, since the text the Vatican released[115] contained no words about apostasy, antipopes, or Antichrist—and in point of fact, *no actual words from the Holy Virgin at all*—a close friend of Ratzinger's decided to confront him. As Fr. Paul Kramer relates in a speech from 2004:

> This professor [Dr. Ingo Dollinger[116]] is a priest that I know personally, and a number of people that I know, know this

---

[113]https://www.vatican.va/roman_curia/congregations/cfaith/documents/rc_con_cfaith_doc_20000626_message-fatima_en.html; How "untimely" since Malachi Martin—one of the few people on earth who seemingly could have confirmed whether this vision was really part or all of the Third Secret—died eleven months earlier (under questionable circumstances).

[114] Ibid.

[115] Cf. Appendix II.

[116] "He...taught moral theology at the seminary of the Order of Canons Regular of the Holy Cross [in Brazil] which belongs to the Opus Angelorum. Bishop Athanasius Schneider, auxiliary bishop of Astana, Kazakhstan, is member of that same Order of Canons Regular of the Holy Cross.

priest personally. He pressed [Ratzinger] on further for an answer, he would not back off. And he demanded, "What is in the Secret? If that's not all of it, well, what is there?" Ratzinger's answer makes it clear. There's no longer any mystery why they have kept it hidden for so many years. And why the Vatican officials, during the pontificate of Pope John XXIII, said in their press release that, "It may never be published," it may not ever be released. Ratzinger said [to Dollinger] that in the Third Secret, Our Lady warns that *there will be an evil council.* And *She warned against the changes*: She warned against making changes in the liturgy; changes in the Mass. This is explicitly set forth in the Third Secret.[117]

Ten years later, in 2010, Ratzinger, now Pope Benedict, once again brought up the contents of the Third Secret—and once more did a complete 180: "We would be mistaken to think that Fatima's prophetic mission is complete."[118]

---

116 (footnote cont'd) Most importantly, Father Dollinger had Padre Pio (d. 1968) as his confessor for many years and became very close to him. Dollinger is also personally known to one of my beloved family members." Maike Hickson, "Cardinal Ratzinger: We Have Not Published the Whole Third Secret of Fatima," *One Peter Five* (May 15, 2016); https://onepeterfive.com/cardinal-ratzinger-not-published-whole-third-secret-fatima/

117 Fr. Paul Kramer "The Imminent Chastisement for Not Fulfilling Our Lady's Request," *Fatima Crusader* 80 (Summer 2005); as cited https://web.archive.org/web/20170404135054/http://www.fatimacrusader.com/cr80/cr80pg32.asp

One day after Gänswein's 2016 Gregorianum Speech (coincidence?), the Vatican issued the following communique: "Several articles have appeared recently, including declarations attributed to Professor Ingo Dollinger according to which Cardinal Ratzinger, after the publication of the Third Secret of Fatima (which took place in June 2000), had confided to him that the publication was not complete. In this regard, Pope emeritus Benedict XVI declares 'never to have spoken with Professor Dollinger about Fatima', clearly affirming that the remarks attributed to Professor Dollinger on the matter 'are pure inventions, absolutely untrue', and he confirms decisively that 'the publication of the Third Secret of Fatima is complete';" https://press.vatican.va/content/salastampa/it/bollettino/pubblico/2016/05/21/0366/00855.html#E

One Peter Five, which had run such articles, responded thusly: https://onepeterfive.wpengine.com/on-fatima-story-pope-emeritus-benedict-xvi-breaks-silence/

118 https://www.vatican.va/content/benedict-xvi/en/homilies/2010/documents/hf_ben-xvi_hom_20100513_fatima.html

Benedict uttered this astonishing about-face during his Pilgrimage Mass at Fatima on May 13th. Two days earlier, during an in-flight press conference he was asked if Fatima's message really was confined to the past:

Reporter: Your Holiness, what meaning do the Fatima apparitions have for us today? In June 2000, when you presented the text of the third secret in the Vatican Press Office, a number of us and our former colleagues were present. You were asked if the message could be extended, beyond the attack on John Paul II, to other sufferings on the part of *the Popes*. Is it possible, to your mind, to include in that vision *the sufferings of the Church today?*

Pope Benedict:...[B]eyond this great vision of the suffering of the Pope, which we can in the first place refer to Pope John Paul II, *an indication is given of realities involving the future of the Church, which are gradually taking shape and becoming evident.* So it is true that, in addition to the moment indicated in the vision, there is mention of, *there is seen, the need for a passion of the Church, which naturally is reflected in the person of the Pope, yet the Pope stands for the Church and thus it is sufferings of the Church that are announced.* The Lord told us that the Church would constantly be suffering, in different ways, until the end of the world...As for the new things which we can find in this message [Fatima Secret] today, there is also the fact that *attacks on the Pope and the Church come not only from without, but the sufferings of the Church come precisely from within the Church, from the sin existing within the Church. This too is something that we have always known, but today we are seeing it in a really terrifying way: that the greatest persecution of the Church comes not from her enemies without, but arises from sin within the Church...*"[119]

It is noteworthy that Ratzinger should cite "sin within the Church." As a young man, he wrote a thesis on the End Times and the Church as understood by the ancient Donatist author, Tyconius (d. 390), in his *Exposition of the Apocalypse*.[120]

As Giorgio Agamben points out:

[Tyconius] distinguishes a dark Church, composed of the *populus malus* of Satan, and a *decora*, honest Church, composed of Christ's faithful. In the present state, the two bodies of the Church are inseparably commingled, but according to the Apostle's prediction, *they will be divided at the end of days*: "Now this goes on from the time of the Lord's passion *until the church, which keeps it in check, withdraws* from the midst of this mystery of lawlessness [*mysterium facinoris*] so that godlessness may be unveiled in its own time"...an eschatological time...goes from Christ's passion up to the "mystery of lawlessness," when the separation of the bipartite body of the Church will be realized...*at the end of the fourth century there were authors who had identified the Church itself as the katechon.*"[121]

---

[119] *Interview of the Holy Father Benedict XVI with the Journalists during the Flight to Portugal* (Papal Flight, 11 May 2010); Cf. https://www.vatican.va/content/benedict-xvi/en/speeches/2010/may/documents/hf_ben-xvi_spe_20100511_portogallo-interview.html.

[120] Joseph Ratzinger, *Beobachtungen zum Kirchenbegriff des Tyconius im Liber regularum, Revue d' Etudes Augustiniennes Et Patristiques* 2 , 1-2 (1956), pp. 173-185. "Reflections on Tyconius's Concept of the Church."

[121] Giorgio Agamben, *The Mystery of Evil: Benedict XVI and the End of Days*, (Stanford, CA: Stanford University Press, 2017). (*Il mistero del male: Benedetto XVI e la fine dei tempi*, Roma-Bari: Gius. Laterza & Figli, 2013).

As Pope, Ratzinger returned to the subject at one of his General Audiences and he specifically mentions that Tyconius "sees the Apocalypse above all as a reflection of the mystery of the Church. Tyconius had reached the conviction that the Church was a bipartite body: on the one hand, he says, she belongs to Christ, but *there is another part of the Church that belongs to the devil.*"[122] Or as he wrote decades earlier, Tyconius argues that the separation of the good from the bad will immediately precede the coming of Antichrist: "*[T]he Antichrist belongs to the Church, grows in it and with it until **the great discessio** [schism/rebellion], which initiates the final revelatio.*"[123]

Archbishop Fulton Sheen
Antichrist and Antichurch

Do we have additional testimony as to the signs of the coming of the Antichrist and his Antichurch?

Venerable Archbishop Fulton J. Sheen once said that when he comes, the Antichrist will, of course, not be called by that title. Neither will he "carry a trident nor wave an arrowed tail." He will not resemble any cartoon devil we have ever seen because as Scripture assures us, he will almost be able to "deceive even the elect" into thinking he is a holy savior. How then shall we recognize him for the villain that he is, if his outward appearance is so magnanimous that we might mistake him for Our Lord? Sheen identifies many characteristics that will give him (and his henchmen) away:

---

[122] *General Audience: Ambrose Autpert* (22 April 2009); Cf. https://www.vatican.va/content/benedict-xvi/en/audiences/2009/documents/hf_ben-xvi_aud_20090422.html.

[123] Joseph Ratzinger, *Observations on Tyconius' Concept of the Church*, 1956.

[I]f there i no sin, then there is no judge, and if there is no judgment then evil is good and good is evil.[124] *But above all these descriptions, Our Lord tells us that he will be so much like Himself that he would deceive even the elect...* How will he come in this new age to win followers to his religion?

...[H]e will come disguised as the Great Humanitarian; he will talk peace, prosperity and plenty not as means to lead us to God, but *as ends in themselves; he will write books on the new idea of God, to suit the way people live...make men shrink in shame if their fellowmen say they are not broadminded and liberal; he will be so broadminded as to identify tolerance with indifference to right and wrong, truth and error; he will spread the lie that men will never be better until thy make society better and thus have selfishness to provide fuel for the next revolution; ...he will foster more divorces under the disguise that another partner is "vital";*[125] he will increase love for love and decrease love for person; *he will invoke religion to destroy religion;* ...he will say his mission is to liberate men from the servitude of superstition and Fascism; he will organize children's games, *tell people whom they should and should not marry and unmarry, who should bear children and who should not;*

...He will tempt Christians with the same three temptations with which he tempted Christ."

---

[124] Cf. Bergoglio's infamous 2013 statement regarding the sin of sodomy among the clergy: "Whom am I to judge?" https://www.nbcnews.com/news/world/who-am-i-judge-popes-most-powerful-phrase-2013-flna2d11791260

[125] Cf. Bergoglio's *Amoris Laetitia* and his "streamlining" of annulment procedures.

...In the midst of all his seeming love for humanity and his glib talk of freedom and equality, he will have one great secret which he will tell to no one: he will not believe in God. *Because his religion will be brotherhood without the fatherhood of God, he will deceive even the elect. He will set up a counter-church which will be the ape of the Church because he, the Devil, is the ape of God. It will have all the notes and characteristics of the Church, but in reverse and emptied of its divine content. It will be a mystical body of the Antichrist that will in all externals resemble the mystical body of Christ.*"[126]

And if these are the qualities of Antichrist and Antichurch, we should also look for them in his herald, the "False Prophet." The Apocalypse makes it clear that just as Jesus had his John the Baptist, so the Lawless One shall have a forerunner.[127] When the Katechon is out of the way, we can expect the arrival of the False Prophet. According to Fr. E. Sylvester Berry, the Papacy may very well be the Katechon:

The words of St. Paul to the Thessalonians may be a reference to *the Papacy as the obstacle to the coming of Antichrist:* "*You know what withholdeth, that he may be revealed in his time. For the mystery of iniquity already worketh; only that he who now holdeth, do hold, until he be taken out of the way. And then that wicked one shall be revealed.*" (2 Thess. 2: 6-7)

---

[126] Archbishop Fulton J. Sheen, "Signs Of Our Times": Ven. Fulton Sheen on Anti-Christ & Crisis in the Church & Society (1947) Andrew Guernsey 'Signs of Our Times' A radio sermon by Ven. Fulton J. Sheen delivered on January 26, 1947; Expanded radio address in transcript printed in 'Signs of Our Times' In *Light Your Lamps*, 8th ed., pp. 5-17. (Huntington, IN: Our Sunday Visitor, 1958): https://goo.gl/y7kROm; Also included in Sheen, *Communism and the Conscience of the West*, (Indianapolis, IN: Bobbs-Merril Company, 1948), pp. 22-25; http://goo.gl/1wQPEs (5:22) http://mediacenter.scdiocese.org/MediaDetail.aspx?ID=70868.OV

[127] Cf. Revelation Chapter 13.

It is a matter of history that the most disastrous periods for the Church were times when the Papal throne was vacant, or *when anti-popes contended with the legitimate head of the Church. Thus also shall it be in those evil days to come.* [128]

Was Benedict then the Katechon? He did tell Seewald that his curious remark when he was first made Pope: "Pray for me that I do not flee for fear of the wolves," was a "fear of this spiritual power of the Antichrist":

Here I must also say that the radius of what a pope may fear is taken to be much too small...the actual threat to the Church and so to the papacy...[comes from] the global dictatorship of ostensibly humanistic ideologies. Contradicting them means being excluded from the basic social consensus. A hundred years ago anyone would have thought it absurd to speak of homosexual marriage. Today anyone opposing it is socially excommunicated. The same goes for abortion and the creation of human beings in laboratories. Modern society is formulating *an antichristic faith, which you cannot oppose without being punished with social excommunication. It is only natural to fear this spiritual power of Antichrist, and it really needs help from the prayers of a whole diocese [Rome?], and the universal Church, to oppose and resist it.*"[129]

According to Fr. Herman Bernard Kramer:

...Our Divine Savior has a representative on earth in the person of the Pope upon whom He has conferred full powers to teach and govern. Likewise, Antichrist will have

---

[128] Rev. E. Sylvester Berry, *The Apocalypse of St. John*, (Columbus, OH: The Catholic Church Supply House, 1921), pp. 120-138.

[129] Seewald, *Benedict XVI: A Life, Vol 2*, pp. 534-535; My translation in a couple of instances.

his representative in the false prophet who will be endowed with the plenitude of satanic powers to deceive the nations.

… As indicated by the resemblance to a lamb, *the prophet will probably set himself up in Rome as a sort of antipope* during the vacancy of the papal throne…

…Antichrist and his prophet will introduce ceremonies to imitate the Sacraments of the Church. In fact there will be a complete organization—a church of Satan set up in opposition to the Church of Christ. Satan will assume the part of God the Father; Antichrist will be honored as Savior, and *his prophet will usurp the role of Pope.* Their ceremonies will counterfeit the Sacraments…"

As a dragon, Satan through the evil world-powers of that time will enter the Church, interfere with her liberty and perhaps by stealthy suggestions having long before directed the choosing of candidates for the episcopate will now endeavor by threats of force to hinder the election of the worthiest candidate for the papacy…

…Though he poses as a lamb, a Christian, his doctrines betray him for he preaches the doctrines of the dragon.

His preaching may be Communism or idolatrous paganism; it will comprise emperor worship and devil worship coupled with persecution of true believers. **They will know him at once as an imposter and will not be misled.**[130]

---

130 Rev. Herman Bernard Kramer, *The Book of Destiny*, (Belleville, IL: Buechler Publishing Company, [reprinted by TAN Books, Rockford Illinois], 1955), pp.77-85; pp. 318-319. NB. "They will know him," they won't need a Church council to inform them.

During the Counter Reformation, the editors of the first modern English translation of the Latin Vulgate Bible once commented:

Not as though he should be a chief member of the Church of Christ, or a special part of his body mystical, and be Antichrist and yet withal continuing within the Church of Christ, as the Heretics feign, to make the Pope Antichrist (whereby they plainly confess and agnise [recognize] that the Pope is a member of the Church, & *in ipso sinu Ecclesia, and in the very bosom of the Church,* say they:) for that is ridiculous, that all Heretics whom St. John calleth Antichrists as his precursors, should go out of the Church, and the great Antichrist himself should be of the Church, and in the Church, and continue in the same. And yet to them that make the whole Church in revolt from God, this is no absurdity.

But the truth is, that this Antichristian revolt here spoken of, is from the Catholic Church: and Antichrist, if he ever were of or in the Church, *shall be an Apostate and a renegade out of the Church, and he shall usurp upon it by tyranny, and by challenging worship, religion, and government thereof,* so that himself shall be adored in all the Churches of the world which he list to leave standing for his honor. And this is to sit in the temple or against the Temple of God, as some interpret. *If any Pope did ever this, or shall do, then let the Adversaries call him Antichrist.*[131]

---

[131] *1582 Rheims New Testament.*

Definition of Heresy

Could Pope Francis be the False Prophet forerunner of the Antichrist? Is he a heretic? Do laymen even have the right to suspect him of such things?

First, we need to define heresy. According to Canon Law:

Can. 750 §1. A person must believe with *divine and Catholic faith* [*de Fide*] all those things contained in the word of God, written or handed on, that is, in the one deposit of faith entrusted to the Church, **and at the same time** *proposed as divinely revealed either by the solemn magisterium of the Church or by its ordinary and universal magisterium*[132] which is manifested by the common adherence of the Christian faithful under the leadership of the sacred magisterium; therefore all are bound to avoid any doctrines whatsoever contrary to them.

Canon 751: *"Heresy is the obstinate denial or obstinate doubt after the reception of baptism of some truth which is to be believed by divine and Catholic faith...."*[133]

As Berry points out:

A doctrine contrary to revealed truth is usually stigmatized as heretical, but a person who professes a heretical doctrine is not necessarily a heretic. *Heresy,* from the Greek *hairesis,* signifies a *choosing;* therefore a heretic is one

---

[132] A list of 238 *De Fide* teachings are found here: https://padreperegrino.org/2022/10/infallible/

[133] "Now, in matters of faith, the will assents to some truth, as to its proper good, as was shown above... Therefore heresy is a species of unbelief, belonging to those who profess the Christian faith, but corrupt its dogmas." *Summa Theologica,* II-II, Q. 11, A 1 and 2; Cf. https://ronconte.com/2021/08/25/in-defense-of-fr-kramer-on-never-failing-faith/

who chooses for himself in matters of faith, thereby rejecting the authority of the Church established by Christ to teach all men the truths of revelation. He rejects the authority of the Church by following his own judgment or by submitting to an authority other than that established by Christ...

A person may reject the teaching authority of the Church knowingly and willingly, or he may do it through ignorance. In the first case he is a *formal* heretic, guilty of grievous sin: in the second case he is a *material* heretic, free from guilt. Both formal and material heresy may be *manifest* [public] or *occult* [hidden, kept to oneself].[134]

Fr. James Schall once wrote: "Heretical popes? The essence of Catholicism is that there be none. It is also its essence that, if necessary, the issue be faced squarely and judged fairly."[135]

The Layman Who Judged His Bishop

But can a layperson accuse a pope using his own private judgement? In fact, there is precedent; there is a prominent example from history of a layman calling out the Patriarch of Constantinople (capital city of the empire). In the early fifth century, Eusebius, a lawyer in the service of the Empress (either Pulcheria or Eudocia), was the first to speak publicly against the teachings of his bishop Nestorius:

The public resistance to Nestorius' teaching culminated when a man of "great erudition and fiery character", as [Saint] Cyril describes him, interrupted one of the sermons

---

[134] Rev. E. Sylvester Berry, *The Church of Christ: An Apologetic and Dogmatic Treatise*, (Emmitsburg, MD: Mount St Mary's Seminary, 1955), p. 128.

[135] Rev. James Schall, "On Heretical Popes," *The Catholic Thing* (Nov. 11, 2014); https://www.thecatholicthing.org/2014/11/11/on-heretical-popes-3/

of the new archbishop exclaiming that the same pre-eternal *Logos* [God the Son] had been born for the second time. This man was the learned Constantinopolitan lawyer Eusebius who was later elected bishop of Dorylaeum. The significance of this statement lies in its emphasis on the divinity of Christ, by virtue of which the Blessed Virgin could be called *Theotokos* [Mother of God]. Thus Eusebius directly challenged not only Nestorius, but the Christological tradition predominant in Antioch, that laid stress on the concreteness of Christ's humanity. [136]

Calling out Nestorius during an heretical sermon was just the first step.

Eusebius' interruption was accepted enthusiastically, which probably encouraged him to further action. One document in connection to the 'Nestorian' controversy authored by Eusebius survives. It is the famous pamphlet *Contestatio Eusebii* in which the author attempted to discredit what he understood to be Nestorius' theology. Originally, it was published anonymously, however the pamphlet can be found in different collections of the Acts of Ephesus (431) where it is invariably ascribed to Eusebius. The full text of the pamphlet survives among the writings of Leontius of Byzantium, who also ascribes it to Eusebius. Eusebius' authorship of the *Contestatio* is universally accepted by the modern scholarship. The text of the *Contestatio* contains six theological statements in which the Christology of Nestorius is presented as strikingly similar to that of [the heretic] Paul of Samosata.[137]

---

[136] Vasilije Vranic, "The Christology of Eusebius of Dorylaeum in the Nestorian Controversy," *Theologicon*, vol. 6., no. 1 (Sept. 27, 2019).

[137] Ibid.

Eusebius posted his document "in public and in the church [Hagia Sophia Cathedral]" which began as follows:

I have sworn this statement by the Holy Trinity so that it may be made known to the bishops, priests, deacons, readers, and the faithful living in Constantinople...that the heresy of Nestorius is of the same kind as that of Paul of Samosata who was condemned 160 years ago by the orthodox fathers.[138]

Him who takes this paper I bind with an oath in the Holy Trinity to *make it known to the bishops, priests and deacons, readers and laypeople living in Constantinople*, and again to make the same public to them for an examination of the heretic Nestorius, since he is like-minded (harmonious) with Paul of Samosata, who was anathematized one hundred and sixty years ago by the orthodox fathers bishops. And this is what each of the two said: (1) Paul said: Mary did not bear *Logos*. (1) Nestorius likewise said: O, the best [of men], Mary did not bear the Godhead. (2) Paul: Neither was she before ages. (2) Nestorius: and they would prefer timely mother to the Godhead, which is the creator of time. (3) Paul: Mary received the *Logos* and was not superior by birth to *Logos*. (3) Nestorius: How then [is it possible that] Mary gave birth to him who was more ancient then herself? (4) Paul: Mary gave birth to a man equal to us. (4) Nestorius: A man was born from the Virgin...

Therefore, if anyone dared to declare that one is the Son who was born consubstantial of the Father before the ages,

---

[138] Timothy E. Gregory, *Vox Populi: Popular Opinion and Violence in the Religious Controversies of the Fifth Century AD*, (Columbus, OH: Ohio State University Press, 1979).

96

and another he who was born of the Virgin Mary, and that it is not one Lord Jesus Christ, let him be anathema!

Eusebius was never sanctioned by the Pope for having the audacity as a layman to resist his Archbishop in the very proactive (and provocative!) way that he did. Indeed, Eusebius was himself later made a bishop and was instrumental in calling out another heresy—Monophysitism.

As for Pope Celestine, in his personal letter to Nestorius, he confirms the "private judgment" of Eusebius and of others who rejected communion with a notorious heretic who had already lost his office by divine sentence:

In your [Nestorius's] letters [to Us] you have made plain the sentence, not so much concerning our Faith, as concerning your own self, since you wish to preach as the word of God something other than that which the Faith of all contains. Behold now what sentence we are obliged to give you; behold the fruits of your novelties. (...) Or will you say to our Lord, "I kept those whom you entrusted to me," when We hear that His Church is torn apart? With what conscience are you living, being *deserted by nearly everyone in this city?* (...) What words can We address you with, in these questions which are blasphemous even to consider? How does it happen that a bishop preaches to the people words which damage the reverence owed to the Virgin Birth? It is not right, that blasphemous words against God should trouble the purity of the ancient Faith. *Was there ever anyone who, adding to or subtracting something from the Faith, was not judged worthy of anathema? For those things which were completely and manifestly handed down to us by the Apostles do not call for addition or subtraction.* (...) Hence, we prepare the heated iron to cauterize these wounds, which, because they merit to be cut off, shall no longer be tolerated. (...) Among the many things which you have wickedly proclaimed, and which *the universal Church repudiates*, we lament the fact that, from the Creed given to us by the Apostles, you have withdrawn the very words which give us the hope of all life and salvation. Why that is so, your own epistles unfold, concerning which there is no doubt that you yourself sent them, and which We were reluctant to take into our hands, lest We be forced to pass judgment on so great a crime. (...)[139]

Eusebius was not alone in calling out Nestorius as a heretic and therefore, no longer bishop of the city:

St Hypatius, a Bithynian monk of the fifth century, insisted on suppressing the name of Nestorius, the patriarch of Constantinople, from the sacred diptychs (equivalent to the Canon of the Mass) from the moment when Nestorius began to preach his heresy, which denied the unity of person in Our Lord. Hypatius's ordinary, the bishop Eulalius (who was a suffragan of Nestorius), refused Nestorius's heresy, but *rebuked the monk for having withdrawn from communion with their patriarch before he had been condemned by a council.* Hypatius replied: "Ever since I learned that Nestorius teaches error about our Lord, I am not in communion with him neither do I include his name in the Eucharistic sacrifice, for he is not a true bishop. Do as you wish to me, for I have made up my mind to suffer all things and nothing will induce me to change my behavior."[140]

---

[139] Translation Fr. MacGillivray; https://sspxpodcast.com/wp-content/uploads/2022/02/The-Case-of-Nestorius.pdf; Cf. original in Greek and Latin in the *Patrologia Latina* among the letters and decrees of Pope St. Celestine I and of Sixtus III: https://www.mlat.uzh.ch/index.php?app=browser

[140] *An Extract from the Life of Saint Hypatius* translated by Ron Conte from the original fifth-century Greek of the monk Callinicus; https://romeward.com/articles/239752647/can-a-private-individual-recognize-an-uncondemned-heretic

To those who would object that Nestorius was just an archbishop and not a pope, so this precedent does not apply, the case of Pope Liberius (r. 352-366) is instructive. He was exiled by an Arian Christian emperor and replaced with antipope Felix. Some sources claim that after two years of deprivation, he reluctantly signed a Semi-Arian formula stating that Christ was of a "similar" substance as the Father, instead of the "same" substance, as the Council of Nicaea had solemnly defined in 325.

St. Robert Bellarmine and Archbishop Vigano
On a Heretical Pope

This is how Doctor of the Church, St. Robert Bellarmine approached the subject of heresy and loss of office with regard to Pope Liberius:

Then indeed the Roman clergy, stripping Liberius of his pontifical dignity, went over to Felix, whom they knew [then] to be a Catholic. From that time, Felix began to be the true Pontiff. For *although Liberius was not a heretic, nevertheless he was considered one*, on account of the peace he made with the Arians, and *by that presumption the pontificate could rightly [merito] be taken from him: for men are not bound, or able to read hearts; but when they see that someone is a heretic by his external works, they judge him to be a heretic pure and simple [simpliciter], and condemn him as a heretic.*[141]

Following Bellarmine's teaching (and the example of the Roman clergy in the mid-fourth century) a lay person would seemingly be quite justified in "judging" Bergoglio a heretic— even if it turned out he was NOT!

---

[141] http://strobertbellarmine.net/bellarm.htm

Now personally, Bellarmine thought it was impossible that God would ever allow a pope to become a heretic, but for the sake of argument, he discussed the subject even further. He took issue with the teaching of Dominican theologian Thomas Cajetan, who claimed that the Church must first officially judge a pope (not lay folk) before he actually loses office:

The fourth opinion is that of Cajetan, for whom[142]...the manifestly heretical Pope is not "*ipso facto*" deposed, but can and must be deposed by the Church. To my judgment, *this opinion cannot be defended*. For, in the first place, it is proven with arguments from authority and from reason that the manifest heretic is "*ipso facto*" deposed. The argument from authority is based on St. Paul (Titus, c. 3), who orders that the heretic be avoided after two warnings, that is, after showing himself to be manifestly obstinate— which means before any excommunication or judicial sentence. And this is what St. Jerome writes, adding that the other sinners are excluded from the Church by sentence of excommunication, but the heretics exile themselves and separate themselves by their own act from the body of Christ. *Now, a Pope who remains Pope cannot be avoided, for how could we be required to avoid our own head? How can we separate ourselves from a member united to us?*

This principle is *most certain*. The non-Christian cannot in any way be Pope, as Cajetan himself admits (ib. c. 26). The reason for this is that he cannot be head of what he is not a member; now he who is not a Christian is not a member of the Church, and a manifest heretic is not a Christian[143]... *therefore the manifest heretic cannot be Pope...the Holy*

---

[142] *De auctor. papae et con.*, cap. 20 et 21.

[143] "as is clearly taught by St. Cyprian (lib. 4, epist. 2), St. Athanasius (Scr. 2 *cont. Arian.*), St. Augustine (*lib. de great. Christ.* cap. 20), St. Jerome (*contra Lucifer.*) and others;"

100

Fathers teach unanimously not only that heretics are outside of the Church, but also that they are "ipso facto" deprived of all ecclesiastical jurisdiction and dignity...[144]

As Pope St. Celestine wrote:[145] "It is evident that he [whoever has been excommunicated by Nestorius] has remained and remains in communion with us, and that we do not consider destituted [i.e. deprived of office, by judgment of Nestorius], anyone who has been excommunicated or deprived of his charge, either episcopal or clerical, by Bishop Nestorius or by the others who followed him, *after they commenced preaching heresy. For he who had already shown himself as deserving to be excommunicated, could not excommunicate anyone by his sentence."*[146]

Then there is the testimony of Pope Adrian II whose decrees from the Council of Rome (869) were read aloud at the Ecumenical Council of Constantinople IV (869):

Although we have read of the Roman pontiff having passed judgement on the bishops of all the churches, *we have not read of anyone having passed judgement on him. For even though Honorius was anathematized after this death by the easterners, it should be known that he had been accused of heresy, **which is the only offence where inferiors have the right to***

---

[144] "St. Cyprian (lib. 2, epist. 6) says: 'We affirm that absolutely no heretic or schismatic has any power or right'; and he also teaches (lib. 2, epist. 1) that the heretics who return to the Church must be received as laymen, even though they have been formerly priests or bishops in the Church. St. Optatus (lib. 1 *cont. Parmen.*) teaches that heretics and schismatics cannot have the keys of the kingdom of heaven, nor bind nor loose. St. Ambrose *(lib. 1 de poenit.,* ca. 2), St. Augustine *(in Enchir.,* cap 65), St. Jerome *(lib. cont. Lucifer.)* teach the same."

[145] *Epist. ad Jo. Antioch.,* which appears in *Conc. Ephes.,* tom. I, cap. 19.

[146] "St. Nicholas I (*epist. ad Michael*) repeats and confirms the same. Finally, St. Thomas also teaches (*S. Theol.,* II-II, q. 39, a. 3) that schismatics immediately lose all jurisdiction, and that anything they try to do on the basis of any jurisdiction will be null."

resist the initiatives of their superiors or are free to reject their false opinions.[147]

This is a "mic drop" statement. A pope at a Roman council actually said that subjects have the right to resist popes *accused* of heresy! And this statement by a pope was unanimously approved by the bishops of the Church at a formal ecumenical council!

According to Archbishop Carlo Maria Vigano:

Therefore I do not agree...[with the statement] ["]If infidelity affects this authority [the Pope], only God can intervene.["] Also because even with regard to lower levels of authority it becomes difficult to have recourse to them and hope to have justice.

The Lord can intervene positively in the course of events, manifesting His will in a prodigious way of even just shortening the evildoers' days. But the infidelity of one who is constituted in authority, although it is not able to be judged [juridically] by his subjects, is not for this reason any less culpable, nor can obedience be demanded to illegitimate or immoral orders. The *effect* which this infidelity has on his subjects is one thing, while the *judgment* about this way of acting is another thing, and still another is the *punishment* that it may merit. Thus, if it is not up to the subjects to put the Pope to death for heresy (despite the death penalty being considered by Saint Thomas Aquinas as commensurate to the crime of one who corrupts the Faith), *we can nevertheless recognize a Pope as a heretic, and as such refuse, on a case-by-case basis, to show him the obedience to which he would otherwise be entitled. We do not judge him, because we do not have the authority to*

[147] *Acts of Constantinople IV*, ed. Leonardi, 238.

do so, but we recognize him for who he is, waiting for Providence to arouse those who can pronounce it definitively and authoritatively.[148]

Bellarmine would take issue with Vigano's assertion that an heretical pope can still be pope in any sense. More recently, Vigano has perhaps adjusted his thinking:

The Church is not a society governed by an absolute monarch, free from any higher authority and able to impose his whims on his subjects. The Head of the Church is Christ, and Christ is her only true King and Lord, of whom the Pope is Vicar, as he is Successor to the Prince of the Apostles. *When one abuses the vicarious power of Christ and places oneself outside of the succession, by spreading heterodox teachings or by imposing norms related to them, one breaks this inner bond with Christ the Head and with the Church the Mystical Body*. In fact, the vicarious power of the Pope enjoys all the prerogatives of absolute, immediate, and direct authority over the Church only in so far as *salus animarum*, following tradition and faithful to our Lord. Moreover, in the exercise of this authority, the Pope always enjoys the special graces of class within the well-defined limits of this end, while they have no effect when acting against Christ and against the Church. Because of this, Bergoglio's furious attempts, however violent and destructive, will inevitably fail and will surely be declared null and void.[149]

And most recently (and most passionately):

---

[148] Carlo Vigano, "Open Letter to Confused Priests," February 2, 2021; https://remnantnewspaper.com/web/index.php/articles/item/5259-open-letter-to-confused-priests-vigano-on-obedience-resistance-francis-and-vaccines

[149] Carlo Vigano, Interview with *Paix Liturgique* (August 14, 2022); https://www.catholicity.com/vigano/2022-08-14.html

Among the titles of the Roman Pontiff recurs, along with *Christi Vicarius*, that of *Servus servorum Dei* ["Servant of the servants of God"]. While the former has been disdainfully rejected by Bergoglio, his choice to retain the latter sounds like a provocation, as evidenced by his words and deeds. The day will come when the *Presuli* of the Church will be asked to clarify what intrigues and what conspiracies could have led to the Throne him who acts as "Servant of Satan's servants," and why they have fearfully witnessed his intemperances or made themselves accomplices of this **proud heretical tyrant.** Let those who know and who keep silent out of false prudence tremble: by their silence they do not protect the honor of the Holy Church, nor do they preserve the simple ones from scandal. On the contrary, they plunge the Bride of the Lamb into ignominy and humiliation, and turn the faithful away from the Ark of salvation at the very moment of the Flood.[150]

Cardinal Burke and Msgr. Bux
On a Heretical Pope

Cardinal Raymond Burke also affirmed with Bellarmine that a manifestly heretical pope would *ipso facto* lose his office, and yet, similarly to Cajetan and Vigano, still seems to be waiting for a formal declaration from his brother cardinals. His 2016 interview with *Catholic World Report* went thusly:

CWR: Some people are saying that the pope could separate himself from communion with the Church. Can the pope legitimately be declared in schism or heresy?

---

[150] Carlo Vigano, Sermon for the Feast of the Chair of St. Peter in Rome, January 19, 2023; https://www.stilumcuriae.com/vigano-omelia-per-la-cattedra-di-san-pietro-lambita-dallapostasia; My translation from the Italian.

Cardinal Burke: *If a Pope would formally profess heresy he would cease, by that act, to be the Pope. It's automatic.* And so, that could happen.

CWR: That could happen.

Cardinal Burke: Yes.

CWR: That's a scary thought.

Cardinal Burke: It is a scary thought, and I hope we won't be witnessing that at any time soon.

CWR: Back to this question about the Pope committing heresy. What happens then, if the Pope commits heresy and is no longer Pope? Is there a new conclave? Who's in charge of the Church? Or do we just not even want to go there to start figuring that stuff out?

Cardinal Burke: There is already in place the discipline to be followed when the Pope ceases from his office, even as happened when Pope Benedict XVI abdicated his office. The Church continued to be governed in the interim between the effective date of his abdication and the inauguration of the papal ministry of Pope Francis.

CWR: Who is competent to declare him to be in heresy?

Cardinal Burke: It would have to be members of the College of Cardinals.[151]

Msgr. Nicola Bux agrees with Burke:

---

[151] "Cardinal Burke: 'No, I am not saying that Pope Francis is in heresy'," *Catholic World Report* (Dec. 19, 2016); https://www.catholicworldreport.com/2016/12/19/cardinal-burke-no-i-am-not-saying-that-pope-francis-is-in-heresy/

Every faithful, including the Pope, if he embraces heresy, separates himself from the unity of the Church. It is well known that the Pope is at the same time a member and a part of the Church, because the hierarchy is within and not above the Church, as stated in *Lumen gentium* (No. 18).

Faced with this eventuality, so serious for the faith, some cardinals, or even the Roman clergy or the Roman synod, could admonish the Pope with fraternal correction, could "resist him in the face" as Paul did with Peter at Antioch; they could refute him and, if necessary, call on him to repent. *Should the Pope be pertinacious in error, it would be necessary to distance oneself from him, in accordance with what the Apostle says (see Titus 3: 10-11).* Furthermore, his heresy and his unwillingness to repent should be declared publicly, so that he might not cause harm to others and so that everyone may protect themselves.

If a heresy were well-known and made public, the Pope would ipso facto lose his pontificate. For theology and canon law, the pertinacious heretic is someone who questions a truth of faith consciously and voluntarily, that is, with the full awareness that this truth is a dogma and with the full adherence of the will.

I note that one can have obstinacy or pertinacity in a sin of heresy committed even simply due to weakness.

Moreover, if the Pope did not want to maintain union and communion with the whole body of the Church, as when he tried to excommunicate the whole Church or to subvert the liturgical rites based on the apostolic tradition, he could be schismatic.

If the Pope does not behave like a Pope and head of the Church, neither is the Church in him nor is he in the Church.[152]

But if we are looking for perhaps an even stronger authority that an heretical pope is no pope at all, we can look to the testimony of Archbishop Purcell, one of the Council Fathers at Vatican I:

The question was also raised by a Cardinal, "What is to be done with the Pope if he becomes a heretic?" It was answered that there has never been such a case; the Council of Bishops could depose him for heresy, *for from the moment he becomes a heretic he is not the head or even a member of the Church. The Church would not be, for a moment, obliged to listen to him when he begins to teach a doctrine the Church knows to be a false doctrine, and he would cease to be Pope, being deposed by God Himself.*

If the Pope, for instance, were to say that the belief in God is false, you would not be obliged to believe him, or if he were to deny the rest of the creed, "I believe in Christ," etc. The supposition is injurious to the Holy Father in the very idea, but serves to show you the fullness with which the subject has been considered and the ample thought given to every possibility. *If he denies any dogma of the Church held by every true believer, he is no more Pope than either you or I;* and so in this respect the dogma of infallibility amounts to nothing as an article of temporal government or cover for heresy.[153]

---

[152] https://insidethevatican.com/news/newsflash/letter-76-the-brux-interview/

[153] Archbishop of Cincinnati, John B. Purcell, quoted in Rev. James J. McGovern, *Life and Life Work of Pope Leo XIII*, (Chicago, IL: Allied Printing, 1903), p. 241.

Rahner and Van Noort
Material Heresies of Pope Francis

If this teaching is true, then as Dr. Taylor Marshall recently put it: "How is this man [Pope Francis] the Vicar of Christ?"[154] In his Abu Dhabi "Declaration on Human Fraternity" of February 4, 2019, he declared (in union with a grand imam!):

The pluralism and *the diversity of religions,* color, sex, race and language *are willed by God* in His wisdom, through which He created human beings...This *divine wisdom is the source from which the right to freedom of belief* and the *freedom to be different derives.* Therefore, the fact that people are forced to adhere to a certain religion or culture must be rejected, as too the imposition of a cultural way of life that others do not accept.[155]

It is material heresy to claim that God wills the diversity of religions. (It is also erroneous to teach that individuals have the God-given right to practice erroneous beliefs and may not be forced in matters of religion.) So how can anyone consider Jorge Bergoglio anything other than a public material heretic, and therefore, not a member of the visible Church? But if he were not a member of the visible Church, he would be an incapable subject of the office of the Roman Pontiff: he could not be Pope.

Let us cite further, perhaps the most cited theologian of the 20th century, Karl Rahner:

...even those *public heretics* and schismatics who either *cannot be proved to be,* or in fact, *are not in heresy* or

---

[154] Taylor Marshall, "Pope Francis wants to legalize Sodomy;" https://www.youtube.com/watch?v=v7t36Oc6nFQ

[155] https://www.vatican.va/content/francesco/en/travels/2019/outside/documents/papa-francesco_20190204_documento-fratellanza-umana.html

schism through formal sin or subjective guilt _are outside the Church_. In short, even heretics and schismatics in good faith...*do not belong as members to the visible Church...* Moreover, *a bishop or Pope*, according to *the universal teaching* and one which is necessary for the steady and sure continuance of ecclesiastical authority, keeps his ecclesiastical powers even if he is *occultly unbelieving*[156] in the purely *internal forum* [i.e. in his heart, not public]. But *possession of ordinary ecclesiastical authority and non-membership in the Church are mutually exclusive notions.*[157]

So Rahner is saying that the unanimous teaching of the theologians is that a public material heretic is not a member of the visible Church and that a bishop or pope in such a case would lose his office *ipso facto*.

Msgr. G. Van Noort concurs:

[I]f public material heretics remained members of the Church, the visibility and unity of Christ's Church would

---

[156] "This crime [public heresy or apostasy] presupposes not an internal, or even external but occult act, but a public defection from the faith through formal heresy, or apostasy, *with or without affiliation with another religious society...*The public character of this crime must be understood in the light of canon 2197 n. 1 [1917 Code of Canon Law]. Hence, if a bishop were guilty of this violation and the fact were divulged to the greater part of the town or community, the crime would be public and the see *ipso facto* [by that very fact] becomes vacant."

"[W]hen a bishop tacitly resigns, as in the case of apostasy, heresy, etc., the see becomes fully vacant the *moment the crime becomes public*. According to a strict interpretation of the law, the jurisdiction of the bishop passes at that moment to the Board [of Diocesan Consultors], who may validly and licitly begin to exercise its power, as long as there is certainty that the crime has become public. In practice, however, it would probably be more prudent on the part of the Board, instead of assuming the governance of the see immediately, to notify the Holy See without delay, and await for such provisions which the Supreme Authority might choose to make." Rev. Leo Arnold Jaeger, *The Administration of Vacant and Quasi-Vacant Dioceses in the United States*, (Washington, D.C.: The Catholic University of America Press, 1932), pp. 82; 98.

[157] Karl Rahner, "Die Zugehörigkeit zur Kirche nach der Lehre der Enzyklika Pius XII *Mystici Corporis Christi*," *Zeitschrift für katholische Theologie*, 69 Band (1947), pp. 129-188.

perish. If these purely material heretics were considered members of the Catholic Church in the strict sense of the term, how would one ever locate the 'Catholic Church'? How would the Church be one body? How would it profess one faith? Where would be its visibility? Where its unity? For these and other reasons we find it difficult to see any intrinsic probability to the opinion which would allow for *public heretics, in good faith,* remaining members of the Church.[158]

In addition to his Abu Dhabi declaration, there are other statements from Bergoglio that qualify as public material heresy. In April 2016, he issued *Amoris Laetitia,* an Apostolic Exhortation in which—in a now infamous footnote—Bergoglio taught that divorced and civilly remarried Catholics without an annulment may receive the sacraments even though they are in a state of objective mortal sin.[159] A few months later, the Conference of Argentine Bishops issued guidelines for Catholics in accordance with this interpretation of *Amoris Laetitia.* Bergoglio then "doubled-down" on his error by publishing a letter to the Argentine bishops "confirming their interpretation of *Amoris Laetitia,*" and then publishing his letter in the *Acta Apostolicae Sedis* (*Acts of the Apostolic See*), the official collection of magisterial decisions and decrees:

The Pope's letter appears in *Acta Apostolicae Sedis* together with the full text of the Argentine bishops' letter. It is also accompanied by a note from Cardinal Pietro Parolin, the

---

[158] G. Van Noort, *Dogmatic Theology,* Vol II. *Christ's Church,* (Westminster, MD, Newman Press, 1957), p. 242.

[159] *Amoris Laetitia,* Chapter 8, Footnote 351: "In some cases this can also include the help of the Sacraments. Accordingly, 'we remind the priests that the confessional should not be a torture chamber, but a place of the Lord's mercy' (Adhort. Ap. *Evangelii Gaudium* [November 24, 2013], 44: *AAS* 105 [2013], 1038). We also say that the Eucharist 'is not the reward of the perfect, but the munificent remedy and sustenance of the weak'" (ibid., 47: 1039).

Vatican Secretary of State, who says that both the papal letter and the bishops' guidelines should be recognized as *acts of the "authentic magisterium."* Cardinal Parolin revealed that the Pontiff had ordered the publication of his letter in the official Vatican gazette.

In his letter, which was originally addressed to the Argentine bishops but became public in September 2016, Pope Francis said that the Argentine guidelines for implementation of *Amoris Laetitia*—which allowed for divorced and remarried Catholics to receive Communion in some cases—reflected an accurate understanding of his apostolic exhortation. "There are no other interpretations," the Pope wrote.[160]

Another example is Bergoglio's teaching on reception of the Eucharist in *Desiderio Desideravi*:

The world still does not know it, but everyone is *invited to the supper of the wedding of the Lamb* (Re 19:9). To be admitted to the feast all that is required is the wedding garment of faith which comes from the hearing of his Word (cf. Rom. 10:17). [Il mondo ancora non lo sa, ma tutti sono *invitati al banchetto di nozze dell'Agnello* (Rev. 19:9). Per accedervi occorre solo l'abito nuziale della fede che viene

---

[160] https://www.catholicculture.org/news/headlines/index.cfm?storyid=34206; as Msgr. Nicola Bux summarizes: "As is well known, the letter of Pope Francis to the Argentine bishops of the Buenos Aires region and the criteria indicated by the latter for access to communion by the divorced and newly married, have been published in *Acta Apostolicae Sedis*, accompanied by a note *ex audientia SS.mi* ["from an audience with the Holy Father"] of the cardinal Secretary of State, who, on the approval of the Pope, considers these two previous documents as an expression of the 'authentic magisterium' of the current Pope and, therefore, as a magisterium to which Catholics must grant pious respect of intellect and will;" as cited https://insidethevatican.com/news/newsflash/letter-76-the-brux-interview/

dall'ascolto della sua Parola (cf. Rm 10:17)[…].¹⁶¹ (emphasis in original)

This contradicts the *De Fide* teaching of the ecumenical Council of Trent:

Chapter VII. The Preparation that Must be Employed to Receive the Holy Eucharist Worthily

If it is not becoming for anyone to approach any of the sacred functions except solemnly, certainly, the more the holiness and the divinity of this heavenly sacrament is understood by a Christian, the more diligently ought he to take heed lest he approach to receive it without great reverence and holiness [can. 2], especially when we read in the Apostle those words full of terror: "He that eateth and drinketh unworthily, eateth and drinketh judgment to himself not discerning the body of the Lord" [1 Cor. 11 :29]. Therefore, the precept, "Let a man prove himself" [1 Cor. 11:28], must be recalled to mind by him who wishes to communicate. Now ecclesiastical usage declares that this examination is necessary, that no one conscious of mortal sin, however contrite he may seem to himself, should

---

¹⁶¹ *Desiderio Desideravi*, 5; https://www.vatican.va/content/francesco/en/apost_letters/documents/20220629-lettera-ap-desiderio-desideravi.html
"On the day that *Desiderio desideravi* was issued, Pope Francis received in audience Nancy Pelosi, the Speaker of the U.S. House of Representatives. Nancy Pelosi has been publicly forbidden to receive communion under Canon 915 by her ordinary, Archbishop Salvatore Cordileone. The grounds for this measure were her consistent political support for the complete legalization of abortion up to birth. After the audience with Pope Francis, Nancy Pelosi received communion at a mass in St. Peter's over which Pope Francis presided, causing scandal to Catholics over all the world. When asked about her illegal reception of communion, Pope Francis expressed no disapproval of it. Instead, he responded by saying 'When the Church loses its pastoral nature, when a bishop loses his pastoral nature, it causes a political problem. That's all I can say.' This response rebukes Archbishop Cordileone for his justified application of Canon 915;" https://www.lifesitenews.com/blogs/bishops-priests-and-scholars-correct-pope-francis-statement-on-holy-communion/

approach the Holy Eucharist without a previous sacramental confession. This, the holy Synod has decreed, is always to be observed by all Christians, even by those priests on whom by their office it may be incumbent to celebrate, provided the recourses of a confessor be not lacking to them. But if in an urgent necessity a priest should celebrate without previous confession, let him confess as soon as possible...

Canon 11. *If anyone says that faith alone is sufficient preparation for receiving the sacrament of the most Holy Eucharist, let him be anathema.* [*Si quis dixerit, solam fidem esse sufficientem praeparationem ad sumendum sanctissimum eucharistiae sacramentum, anathema sit.*][162]

In September 2022, a public document demonstrating the contradiction between Bergoglio's teaching and the infallible teaching of Trent was signed by several bishops:

We, the undersigned, confess the Catholic faith concerning the worthy reception of the Eucharist as it is defined by the Council of Trent, according to which faith alone is not a sufficient preparation for receiving the sacrament of the most Holy Eucharist. We encourage all the bishops and clerics of the Catholic Church to publicly confess the same doctrine about the worthy reception of the Eucharist, and enforce the related canons in order to avoid grave and public scandal.
[Signed.]
Signatories
Most Rev. Joseph Strickland, Bishop of Tyler

---

[162] Council of Trent, October 11, 1551; as cited https://www.lifesitenews.com/wp-content/uploads/2022/09/The-teaching-of-the-Catholic-faith-on-the-reception-of-the-Holy-Eucharist.pdf

Most Rev. René Henry Gracida, Bishop Emeritus of Corpus Christi
Most Rev. Robert Mutsaerts, Auxiliary Bishop of S'Hertogenbosch in Netherlands
Most Rev. Athanasius Schneider, Auxiliary Bishop of Astana, Kazakhstan

Fr. Berry and Cardinal Stickler
On a Heretic Pope

Additional testimony that a public material heretic pope would automatically lose his office is provided by Berry:

Finally, if a pope, in his private capacity as an individual, should fall into manifest heresy, he would cease to be a member of the Church, and in consequence *would also cease to be her supreme pastor*. But this is another purely theoretical hypothesis, since *no Pope is known to have fallen into heresy, and it is most probable that the vicar of Christ is divinely protected from such a misfortune*, although the Church has never defined anything in the matter. "[163]

Fr. Franz Wernz and Fr. Pedro Vidal's *Ius Canonicum*, an eight-volume work published in 1943, which is perhaps the most highly respected commentary on the 1917 Code of Canon Law, states:

Through notorious and openly divulged heresy, *the Roman Pontiff, should he fall into heresy, by that very fact [ipso facto] is deemed to be deprived of the power of jurisdiction even before any declaratory judgement by the Church...A* pope who falls into public heresy would cease *ipso facto* to

---

[163] Berry, *The Church of Christ*, p. 229.

be a member of the Church; therefore, he would also cease to be head of the Church.[164]

This is also confirmed by Ludwig Ott: "Public heretics, *even those who err in good faith* (material heretics), do not belong to the body of the Church, that is, the legal commonwealth of the Church."[165]   And by Van Noort:

Public heretics (and *a fortiori*, apostates) are not members of the Church. They are not members because they separate themselves from the unity of Catholic faith and from the external profession of that faith. Obviously, therefore, they lack one of the three factors – baptism, profession of the same faith, union with the hierarchy – pointed out by Pius XII as requisite for membership of the Church. The same pontiff has explicitly pointed out that, unlike other sins, heresy, schism and apostasy automatically sever a man from the Church. [...]

By the term *public heretics* at this point we mean all who *externally* deny a truth (for example Mary's Divine Maternity), or several truths of divine and Catholic faith, regardless of whether the one denying does so ignorantly and innocently (a merely *material* heretic), or willfully and guiltily (a *formal* heretic).[166]

As Cardinal Billot affirms:

---

[164] Wernz, Vidal, *Ius Canonicum* II, p. 453; As Dr. Edward Peters comments: "I know of no author coming after Wernz who disputes this analysis;" https://canonlawblog.wordpress.com/2016/12/16/a-canonical-primer-on-popes-and-heresy/

[165] Ludwig Ott, *Fundamentals of Catholic Dogma*, (Rockford, IL: Tan Books, 1974), pp. 309-311.

[166] Van Noort, *Christ's Church*, p. 241.

"[N]otorious heretics are excluded from the body of the Church." Some theologians have defended the proposition that *public material* heretics are members of the Church. However, the contrary opinion is the more common opinion of theologians...if public material heretics remained members of the Church, the visibility and unity of Christ's Church would perish. If these purely material heretics were considered members of the Catholic Church in the strict sense of the term, how would one ever locate the 'Catholic Church'? How would the Church be one body? How would it profess one faith? Where would be its visibility? Where its unity? For these and other reasons we find it difficult to see any intrinsic probability to the opinion which would allow for public heretics, in good faith, remaining members of the Church."[167]

Cardinal Alfons Stickler, professor of canon law and church legal history and Archivist and Librarian of the Holy Roman Church explained:

The canonists reflect the *Decretum*, and the *Decretum* reflects the first millennium of the Church; and it is in the light of that tradition that it appears clearly that *the pope stands for the Church which has never erred, which cannot err, in questions that involve eternal spiritual salvation. Therefore, he is the absolute (and, consequently, implicitly infallible) guarantor of the truth which one who wishes to be Catholic must profess...if the pope really errs in matters already defined* (and this is something to be proved because it is often erroneously asserted), *he is no longer pope and therefore does not compromise and cannot compromise papal infallibility.*

---

[167] Berry, *The Church of Christ*, p. 273.

....He and the Church of Rome can never be conceived of as two disjunct or (even less) opposed things: the Roman Pontiff is, in this context, the Church of Rome, and therefore the inerrancy of the Church of Rome is the inerrancy of the Roman Pontiff. If the person of the pope becomes a heretic, he no longer holds the office of pope, just as a judge who has become clinically insane, even though he remains the same person, can no longer be regarded as a judge as far as the effects of the office are concerned. Consequently, *there is no difficulty in referring to the pope, in fact principally to the pope, the affirmation of the same canonists who exclude the possibility of error of the Church of Rome ("quia Deus non permitteret").*[168]

[168] Cardinal Alfons M. Stickler, *The Catholic Historical Review,* vol. 60, no. 3 (October 1974), pp. 427-441; Cf. http://www.obeythepope.com/2017/12/the-indefectible-church-of-rome.html;

Chapter Four
"Duty to Make it Known"

"It should be recognized that the faithful, clerical as well as *lay, have a just freedom of enquiry, of thought and of humble and courageous expression in those matters in which they enjoy competence.*"
Vatican II, *Gaudium et Spes*, 62

"According to the knowledge, competence, and prestige which they possess, they have the right and even at times **the duty to manifest to the sacred pastors their opinion on matters which pertain to the good of the Church and to make their opinion known to the rest of the Christian faithful**, without prejudice to the integrity of faith and morals, with reverence toward their pastors, and attentive to common advantage and the dignity of persons."
Canon 212 §3

"Who's going to save our Church? It's not our bishops, it's not our priests and it is not the religious. It is up to you, the people. You have the minds, the eyes and the ears to save the Church. Your mission is to see that the priests act like priests, your bishops act like bishops, and the religious act like religious."
Servant of God Archbishop Fulton J. Sheen, May 28, 1972

Despite all the evidence presented, Catholics who believe that Benedict may very well have been the legitimate Pope right up until his death are routinely accused of causing scandal and schism. As a prominent Catholic podcaster recently tweeted:

Make no bloody mistake about it, it is an act of schism (and therefore a grave sin) for a Catholic to deny the papacy of

Pope Francis...shame on any Catholic who legitimizes this position, saying that it is within the realm of orthodoxy.[169]

Pope: "It is better that scandal arise than the truth be suppressed."

Because of expressions like this, it seems appropriate to introduce the thoughts of the late Fr. Nicholas Gruner on revealing the truth about the Third Secret of Fatima and giving scandal to others:

The truth is more important than whether it pleases me or not...Is it right for me to say these things?...Is it good for the faithful to hear such things? Even if this is true, will this do harm to the faithful?...This is the dilemma that every priest...and most of them I think make the wrong decision...how can you say these things and be faithful to the Church and faithful to the Pope and love the Church and the faithful?...But it is of no use to the Pope to have sycophants around him congratulating him and telling him he is doing...right when he's doing the absolute wrong thing...I'm not here to judge anyone...but it would be wrong for me...to call evil good and good evil...Our first obligation is to the truth and then to speak the truth and certainly about issues of fundamental morality of good and evil we must speak and speak clearly.

And Scripture itself says "Woe to those who call evil good and good evil"(Isaiah 5:20)...Error has real consequences.. can be lethal...*Is it right for us to maintain silence about these things because it's going to cause some scandal? It's going to upset the faithful? Some faithful might be tempted*

169 Matt Fradd, *Pints With Aquinas* tweet, January 1, 2023; Cf. https://twitter.com/CoffinMedia/status/1610356583946678272

to leave the Church or not practice their faith anymore—that is not the intention of any of this, but as Pope Felix said: "It is better that scandal arise than the truth be suppressed."[170]

The truth is primordial and the message of Our Lady of Fatima who came to pronounce this truth for us, for our day is primordial...how maintain fidelity to the Church... along with knowing the truth...*certainly* [*it is*] *not the intention to have anyone be scandalized to not practice their faith, but it's not my intention to hide the truth in order that we have a day of peace today and have the day of reckoning tomorrow, twice as bad—or worse.*[171]

Under the Pontificate of Leo XIII, the Rev. Felix Sarda y Salvany likewise defended the right of the faithful to use their own (informed) judgement in concrete cases (subject to correction if erroneous):

Of what use would be the rule of faith and morals if in every particular case *the faithful could not of themselves make the immediate application, or if they were constantly obliged to consult the Pope or the diocesan pastor?* Just as the general rule of morality is the law in accordance with which each one squares his own conscience (*dictamen practicum*–"practical judgment") in making particular applications of this general rule (subject to correction if erroneous), so the general rule of faith, which is the infallible authority of the Church, is and ought to be in consonance with every

---

[170] Pope St. Gregory the Great is the actual author of these words, though Pope Felix III spoke in a similar vein: "Not to oppose error is to approve it: and not to defend truth is to suppress it: and indeed to neglect to confound evil men, when we can do it, is no less a sin than to encourage them."

[171] Fr. Nicholas Gruner, "Fatima: Your Last Chance Conference," Rome, May 14-18, 2012; https://www.youtube.com/watch?v=aw6yAfyPJh8&t=3492s

particular judgment formed in making concrete applications–subject, of course, to correction and retraction in the event of [a] mistake in so applying it. It would be rendering the superior rule of faith useless, absurd and impossible to require the supreme authority of the Church to make its special and immediate application in every case and upon every occasion which calls it forth.[172]

Fradd recently had former freemason John Salza on his podcast, who spoke against those "Benevacantists" who believe Benedict was the true pope. Salza advanced the argument that all defects in a papal election are "healed in the root" by the universal acceptance of the Church of that person as pope: "That acceptance is an *infallible* effect of the cause [Christ making him pope because all conditions were met]."[173] Therefore, because only a handful of bishops and not one cardinal, has *publicly* rejected Francis as pope, Benedict could not have been Pope after his resignation.

To answer Salza's argument, let us begin with some background on infallible beliefs, that is, beliefs all Catholics *must* accept.

Truths Divinely Revealed or Proposed by the Church

After 25 years of dissenting priests, theologians and bishops' conferences, Pope John Paul II in 1989, published an authoritative *Profession of Faith*. It begins with the venerable

---

[172] Rev. Felix Sarda y Salvany, *Liberalism is a Sin*, Translated and adapted by Condé B. Pallen (Rockford, IL: TAN Books, 1993), pp. 154-155; "This book was first published in Spanish in 1886 and received the highest praise from the Holy See under Pope Leo XIII;" https://novusordowatch.org/2022/01/kwasniewski-still-lost-in-blunderland-part3/; as cited in Paul Kramer, *To Deceive the Elect*.

[173] Pints with Aquinas, https://www.youtube.com/watch?v=gd0OhVy1JtM&t=9637s

Nicene Creed which Catholics profess every Sunday, but then it adds:

> With firm faith, I also believe everything contained in the word of God, whether written or handed down in Tradition, which the Church, either by a solemn judgment or by the ordinary and universal Magisterium, sets forth to be believed as divinely revealed.

> I also firmly accept and hold each and everything definitively proposed by the Church regarding teaching on faith and morals.

> Moreover, I adhere with religious submission of will and intellect to the teachings which either the Roman Pontiff or the College of Bishops enunciate when they exercise their authentic Magisterium, even if they do not intend to proclaim these teachings by a definitive act.[174]

Nine years later, in the Motu Proprio *Ad Tuendam Fidem*, issued May 18, 1998, Wojtyla draws our attention to

> The second paragraph, however, which states "I also firmly accept and hold each and everything definitively proposed by the Church regarding teaching on faith and morals," has no corresponding canon in the Codes of the Catholic Church. This second paragraph of the Profession of faith is of utmost importance since it refers to *truths that are necessarily connected to divine revelation. These truths*, in the investigation of Catholic doctrine, illustrate the Divine Spirit's particular inspiration for the Church's deeper understanding of *a truth concerning faith and morals, with*

---

[174] https://www.vatican.va/roman_curia/congregations/cfaith/documents/rc_con_cfaith_doc_1998_professio-fidei_en.html

which they are connected either for historical reasons or by a logical relationship.[175]

Such truths, though not divinely revealed, nevertheless are called "dogmatic facts." Indeed, one month later, Ratzinger, then head of the Congregation for the Doctrine of the Faith, explained matters in an official Commentary on the Profession of Faith:

> Such doctrines can be defined solemnly by the Roman Pontiff when he speaks 'ex cathedra' or by the College of Bishops gathered in council, or they can be taught infallibly by the ordinary and universal Magisterium of the Church as a *'sententia definitive tenenda'*. Every believer, therefore, is required to give firm and definitive assent to these truths, based on faith in the Holy Spirit's assistance to the Church's Magisterium, and on the Catholic doctrine of the infallibility of the Magisterium in these matters. *Whoever denies these truths would be in a position of rejecting a truth of Catholic doctrine and would therefore no longer be in full communion with the Catholic Church.*[176]

Since the denial of a truth of this type would result in such a drastic consequence, Ratzinger provides some concrete examples of them:

> With regard to those *truths connected to revelation by historical necessity* and which **are to be held definitively**, but are not able to be declared as divinely revealed, the following examples can be given: **the legitimacy of the election of the Supreme Pontiff**...*the canonizations of saints (dogmatic facts)...*

---

[175] https://www.vatican.va/content/john-paul-ii/en/motu_proprio/documents/hf_jp-ii_motu-proprio_30061998_ad-tuendam-fidem.html

[176] Ibid.

To all intents and purposes then it would certainly appear that *"Roma locuta est!"* All speculation to the contrary of these truths is strictly forbidden on pain of mortal sin and loss of full communion—at least where the electoral legitimacy of a universally accepted pope or the papally promulgated canonization of a saint is concerned.

How shocking then it is to read the following from a recent *One Peter Five* book review by Nicholas Kalinowski:

It would be fair to say that a majority of the small number of Catholics who have even given a moment's thought to the subject believe that canonizations are infallible. However, a growing minority of Catholics are raising questions about and difficulties with this belief. The minority opinion is probably larger than statistics would indicate, because stating this opinion outright might win someone the title of "schismatic" or "heretical" (or that favorite manualist word "temerarious"), endanger a job, or bring sidelong glances from friends.

Besides external considerations, what about one's own soul? Does asserting that canonizations are fallible put a Catholic on the slippery slope to hell? Unfortunately, this crisis of conscience is troubling not a few devout Catholics today, who are disturbed about certain canonizations of recent times and possess an uneasy feeling that something has gone horribly wrong but do not know exactly how to put their finger on what that might be. If you fall into this category, or even if you wish to know why someone might, the recently published book *Are Canonizations Infallible?* will bring peace of mind and shed light on every facet of the question at hand.

If the reader does not want to take someone else's word for it that it is indeed allowable to think canonizations are fallible, he must buckle-up for a detailed theological journey. The editor of the volume, Dr. Peter Kwasniewski, has gathered essays written by twelve historians and theologians who know their material backwards and forwards.[177]

Apparently, questioning whether canonizations are infallible *is allowable after all.*

And by the same logic, questioning the electoral legitimacy of a pope is also allowable, despite what another *One Peter Five* contributor, Robert Siscoe, has (rather categorically) stated:

If we apply this doctrine [universal peaceful acceptance] to Francis, it proves that his election was valid, since the entire Church accepted him as pope following his election. The concerns over the St. Gallen Mafia and Benedict's abdication did not arise until the following year, which was too late. By then, Francis's legitimacy as pope had already been established with infallible certainty. And since the legitimacy of a pope logically proves that all the conditions required for him to have become pope were satisfied, the universal acceptance of Francis following his election proves that Benedict's abdication was accepted by Christ.[178]

Indeed, both Siscoe and his colleague, John Salza have devoted virtually an entire website (and chapters of books) to proclaiming the infallible doctrine of universal peaceful

---

[177] Nicholas Kalinowski, "Are Canonizations Infallible?" *One Peter Five* (November 8, 2021); https://onepeterfive.com/are-canonizations-infallible/

[178] Robert Siscoe, "Dogmatic Fact: The One Doctrine That Proves Francis is Pope," *One Peter Five* (March 18, 2019); https://onepeterfive.com/dogmatic-fact-francis-pope/#_ftnref3

acceptance (UPA) over and against "a growing minority of Catholics who are raising questions about and difficulties with this belief," to use Kalinowski's words: "The minority opinion is probably larger than statistics would indicate, because stating this opinion outright might win someone the title of 'schismatic' or 'heretical' (or that favorite manualist word 'temerarious'), endanger a job, or bring sidelong glances from friends." Such individuals are routinely labeled "Benevacantists" or "Beneplenists,"and summarily dismissed:

> During this time of chaos and doctrinal confusion, the proper response is not to imitate heretics by rejecting "sound doctrine," but rather to stand fast and hold to tradition (Cf. 2 Thess. 2:14), which, as St. Vincent of Lerins said, "can never be led astray by any lying novelty." No one who holds fast to tradition will reject the legitimacy of a pope whose election has been universally accepted by the Church.[179]

But logic is a pesky thing. And as the old adage has it, what is good for the goose—is always good for the gander. If it is allowable to think canonizations are fallible, it is allowable to think that the universal peaceful acceptance of a pope is fallible.

Lest readers think that the book, *Are Canonizations Infallible?* merely contains the rantings of a handful of angry Rad Trads, I should like to point out that in it, no less a personage than Bishop Giuseppe Sciacca, the current Secretary of the Supreme Tribunal of the Apostolic Signatura (the Church's highest court!) is quoted as replying in the following exchange with a *Vatican Insider* reporter:

---

[179] Robert Siscoe, "For Each Objection an Answer: Why Francis is Pope" *One Peter Five* (March 19, 2019); https://onepeterfive.com/objection-answer-francis-pope/

"But there was a doctrinal text issued by the Congregation for the Doctrine of the Faith (CDF) in May 1998 which also mentions infallibility in canonizations."

Sciacca replies: "It is patently clear that the purpose of the [CDF] passage in question is *purely illustrative and is not intended as a definition*. *The recurring argument according to which the Church cannot teach or accept mistakes is intrinsically weak in this case.* But saying that an act is not infallible does not mean to say that the act is wrong or deceiving. Indeed, the mistake may have been made either rarely or never. Canonization, *which everyone admits does not derive directly from faith, is never an actual definition relating to faith or tradition*...[180]

Again, the same logic applies to the CDF's mention of the legitimacy of papal elections. To use Sciacca's words, "it was illustrative and not intended as a definition." One may rightly argue then that in the case of whether a pope is legitimate or not, the near-totality of the bishops of the Church "rarely" make mistakes—but rarely is not the same as never. Furthermore, the electoral legitimacy of a pope "does not derive directly from faith, is never an actual definition relating to faith or tradition," therefore, not an object of infallibility.

On their site, Salza and Siscoe list some 48 authorities mainly from the nineteenth and early twentieth centuries who "taught the doctrine" that universal peaceful acceptance (UPA) of a pope by the bishops infallibly guarantees his legitimacy. This staggering array of authors is an overwhelming display of force obviously intended to disarm any outlier, pea-brained dissenters.

---

[180] Christopher Ferrara, "The Canonization Crisis" in Dr. Peter Kwasniewski, ed. *Are Canonizations Infallible? Revisiting a Disputed Question*, (Arouca Press, 2021). Kindle Edition. (Location 3787)

It makes one think of Fr. Frederick Copleston, the famous Jesuit who wrote the influential multi-volume history of philosophy, and his remark on the weight of arguments from authority according to St. Thomas Aquinas:

Aquinas was the last man to think that philosophical problems can be settled by appeal to great names. "Argument from authority based on human reason is the weakest" (ST, 1a, 1, 8 ad 2). In other words, an argument in favor of a given philosophical or scientific position is the weakest sort of argument when it rests simply on the prestige attaching to the name of an eminent philosopher or scientist. What counts is the intrinsic value of the argument, not the reputation of someone who has sponsored it in the past (Aquinas, 23).[181]

When we examine the intrinsic value of the arguments used by proponents of the infallibility of UPA, there is an astounding lack of argumentation!

Now many of the sources listed by Salza and Siscoe simply teach the existence in Catholic teaching of the category of Dogmatic Facts without actually going into any arguments for UPA. *Virtually all* those who do treat UPA directly resort to the tactic of *reductio ad absurdum* to "prove" their point.

Typical is the reasoning of Hugo Hurter, S.J. in his *Theologiae Dogmaticae Compendium* (1885):

[Dogmatic facts] include things of this sort: that the Sacred Scriptures we use are genuine; that the Councils of Nicaea, Ephesus, Trent, etc. were legitimate; *that Pius IX, Leo XIII,*

[181] https://thomistica.net/news/2011/10/18/aquinas-on-the-epistemology-of-authority.html

etc. were elected legitimately and consequently were legitimate successors to Peter as Bishops of Rome. Just see what would result if you would let any of these things be called into doubt. *Definitions issued during Councils would not have certainty. There would be no sure way of determining the center of Catholic unity. In short, what would result is the uprooting of faith itself and the destruction of Revelation.*[182]

Or of Adolphe Tanquerey's *Dogmatic Theology* (1959):

For if the Church could make a mistake concerning the authority of the Holy Pontiff or of a Council, then *there would always be grounds for doubting whether their decisions were infallible and accordingly for rejecting these decisions.*[183]

And of Cardinal Billot's *De Ecclesia Christi*, Quaestio XIV - *De Romano Pontifice*, Thesis XXIX, §3 (1909):

For the adhesion of the Church to a false Pontiff would be the same as its adhesion to a false rule of faith, seeing that the Pope is the living rule of faith which the Church must follow and which in fact she always follows. As will become even more clear by what we shall say later, God can permit that at times a vacancy in the Apostolic See be prolonged for a long time. He can also permit that doubt arise about the legitimacy of this or that election. He cannot however permit that the whole Church accept as Pontiff him who is not so truly and legitimately.[184]

---

[182] http://www.trueorfalsepope.com/p/peaceful-and-universal-acceptance-quotes.html
[183] Ibid.
[184] Ibid.

These *reductio* arguments are the weakest and therefore the easiest to refute: Having a *legitimate* pope, (Paul VI comes to mind) does not, in fact, guarantee that the doctrinal teaching of Councils will have certainty and lack grounds for doubt! Having a putatively legitimate pope (**Francis** comes to mind) does not ensure Catholic *unity*, nor a *"living rule of faith* which the Church *must* follow and which in fact she *always* follows"! So the universal peaceful acceptance of an illegitimate pope would provide no practical difference.

Indeed, one can argue just as easily—or more so—that God in His Providence would prevent a false pope who was universally peacefully accepted from ever calling a council or binding the faithful in an extraordinary teaching, as arguing the infallibility of the world's bishops on the subject of who the rightful pope is.

Lastly, Salza and Siscoe cite several authors in defense of UPA who seemingly contradict *themselves*. For example, they list Fr. E. Sylvester Berry's *The Church of Christ* (1955), yet he *also* writes:

When there is a prudent doubt about the validity of an election to any official position there is also a similar doubt whether the person so elected really has authority or not. In such a case no one is bound to obey him for it is an axiom that a doubtful law begets no obligation--*lex dubia non obligat*. But a superior whom no one is bound to obey is in reality no superior at all. Hence the saying of Saint Robert Bellarmine [*De Concilio* 2:19] *a doubtful Pope is no Pope*;

And they quote from Wernz and Vidal's *Ius Canonicum,* (1943), but in another place theses canonists also say:

Finally they *cannot be numbered among the schismatics*, who refuse to obey the Roman Pontiff because they consider his *person to be suspect or doubtfully elected* on account of rumours in circulation.[185]

How exactly could someone who denied an infallible truth as Salza and Siscoe claim NOT be a schismatic?

Lastly, if UPA were an infallible truth, how could Cajetan (someone Salza and Siscoe applaud in other contexts) write in his commentary on the *Summa*:

If someone, for a reasonable motive, holds the person of the pope in suspicion and refuses his presence and even his jurisdiction, he does not commit the delict of schism, nor any other whatsoever, provided that he be ready to accept the pope were he not held in suspicion. It goes without saying that one has the right to avoid what is harmful and to ward off dangers. In fact, it may happen that the pope could govern tyrannically, and that is all the easier as he is the more powerful and does not fear any punishment from anyone on earth.[186]

---

[185] Wernz, Vidal, *Ius Canonicum*, 7, p. 398.
https://archive.org/details/IusCanonicumWernzSJVidalSJ/7%20%28Ius%20Poenale%20Ecclesiasticum%29-%20Ius%20Canonicum-%20Wernz%20SJ%2C%20Vidal%20SJ/page/n223/mode/2up

[186] Thomas Cajetan, *Commentary on the Summa Theologiae of St. Thomas Aquinas*; entry on "schism"; https://archive.org/details/operaomniaiussui08thom/page/308/mode/2up

Conclusion

"I do not mean to suggest that Benedict is implying that he will, in some *legal or juridical sense*, remain Pope. But there is an implication here of some kind of *ontological papal residuum*, so to speak, that remains in him even now …[E]lection to the papacy leaves no indelible mark on the soul.
So, why does Benedict thus muddy the waters instead of simply making it clear that he will cease entirely to be Pope — rather than simply losing the power of the office? Do we not see here yet another example of the blurring of concepts that has plagued the Church since Vatican II, or what the genius Romano Amerio called a "loss of essences" — the clear distinction between one thing and another — in post-conciliar thinking?
Must we now accommodate an ambiguity even as to the nature of the papal office? Have we seen the emergence of the latest post-conciliar novelty in the Church: *the quasi-Pope? The 'retired Pope' who in some vague way remains a Pope of sorts?*"[187]
Christopher A. Ferrara, 2013

"One imagines that *the Pope, the representative of Christ on earth,* must have a particularly close, intimate relationship to the Lord."
Peter Seewald 2016

"Yes, it should be that way, *and I do not have the feeling that he is far away.* [**Present tense**] *I am always able to speak with him inwardly*. But I am, nevertheless, just a lowly little man who does not always reach all the way up to him." [188]
Pope Benedict 2016

---

[187]https://web.archive.org/web/20170615133649/http://www.fatimaperspectives.com/oc/perspective654.asp

[188] Seewald says, "**the Pope** must have a close relationship to the Lord." Benedict answers, "**I do** not have the feeling He **is** far away. I **am** always able to speak to Him." …

133

In *Last Testament*, Pope Benedict admonished Peter Seewald: *"The follower of Peter* is not merely bound to a function;" This statement means there is more to being a successor of St. Peter than the functional "ministry of the bishop of Rome;" this something "more" that Benedict believed himself still bound to is *that which he never renounced*; by his own admission, metaphysically, he could not: "the office [*munus*] enters into your very being;" or as Gänswein avowed: *"he has not abandoned the Office of Peter [Munus Petrinum] — something which would have been entirely impossible for him after his irrevocable acceptance of the office in April 2005,",* "now [2016] we have had for three years *two popes* and I have the impression that the reality that I perceive is covered by what I have said."

So in the end, it does not matter if Benedict went to his grave considering Francis to be the one and only Pope (i.e. active bishop of Rome), Benedict still esteemed himself an ontologically current, not former "successor of Peter." As Gänswein said: "As in the time of Peter, also today the one, holy, catholic, and apostolic Church continues to have one legitimate Pope [Francis]. But today we live with *two living successors of Peter among us.*"[189]

Therefore, I submit that the object of Benedict's renunciation was erroneously understood by him, which

---

[188] (Footnote cont'd) Not "**I did** not have the feeling He **was** far away [back when I <u>was</u> Pope]. I **was** always able to speak to Him." Benedict answers as Pope—in the present tense! Their exchange In the original German: Seewald: „Man stellt sich vor, der Papst, Stellvertreter Christi auf Erden, müsste ein besonders enges, intimes Verhältnis zum Herrn haben." Benedict: „Ja, das sollte so sein, und ich habe auch nicht das Gefühl, dass Er weit weg ist. Ich kann innerlich immer mit Ihm reden. Aber trotzdem bin ich halt ein armseliger kleiner Mensch, der bis zu Ihm nicht immer hinaufreicht."

[189] This sentiment was recently echoed by Cardinal Becciu: *"Con la morte di Papa Benedetto, ecco, adesso abbiamo un papa, e questo è il papa della Chiesa."* "With the death of Pope Benedict, look, now we have one pope, and this pope is the Pope of the Church;" https://www.iene.mediaset.it/video/scandalo-in-vaticano-becciu_1199426.shtml Becciu's implied meaning: "We had two popes, with the death of Benedict...now we're down to one."

according to both canon law (Canon 188) and Natural Law, makes his renunciation invalid.

Let it also be noted that in addition to dozens of competent laypersons, at least two prominent prelates have called for an inquiry into Pope Benedict's renunciation. Msgr. Bux, for example, one of Ratzinger's closest collaborators as consultor to the Office of Liturgical Celebrations of the Supreme Pontiff and Causes of Saints. In an interview with author and blogger Aldo Maria Valli published October 13, 2018, speaking of solutions to the crisis in the Church, Bux said we ought to

> *study more accurately the question concerning the juridical validity of Pope Benedict XVI's renunciation, i.e., whether it was full or partial ("halfway," as some have said) or doubtful, since the idea of a sort of collegiate papacy seems to me decidedly against the Gospel text.* In fact, Jesus did not say "*Tibi dabo claves...*" ["I will give to you the keys"] turning to Peter and Andrew, but he only told Peter! That's why I say that, *perhaps, a thorough study of the resignation could be more useful and profitable,* as well as helping to overcome problems that today seem insurmountable to us.[190]

In another interview with Valli published April 5, 2022, Archbishop Vigano seconded Bux's call, stating that before another conclave can be held, it will be necessary for the Church to investigate the abdication of Benedict XVI and the 2013 Conclave that elected Francis:

> But before discussing the next conclave, *it is necessary to shed light on the abdication of Benedict XVI* and on the question of the frauds of the 2013 Conclave, which sooner

---

[190] https://insidethevatican.com/news/newsflash/letter-76-the-bux-interview/

or later will have to give rise to an official investigation. If there were to be proofs of irregularity, the conclave would be null, the election of Bergoglio null, just as all his appointments, acts of government and magisterium would be null. A reset that would providentially bring us back to the *status quo ante*, with a College of Cardinals composed only of cardinals appointed up to Benedict XVI, ousting all those created since 2013, notoriously ultra-progressive. *Certainly, the current situation, with all the rumors about Ratzinger's resignation and Bergoglio's election, does not help the ecclesial body and creates confusion and disorientation in the faithful."*[191]

Whenever that future commission meets, its judgment on the validity of Ratzinger's renunciation may well hinge on the orthodoxy or heterodoxy of his statement: "The follower of Peter is not merely bound to a function...Fulfilling a function is not the only criterion [for being Pope]." No longer functioning as Bishop of Rome then, was for Ratzinger apparently no impediment to his ongoing status as Successor of St. Peter—the irrevocable "Pope" in Pope Emeritus. But if he erred substantially, then not only was he still Successor of St. Peter, he was still the only legitimate Pope.

The Katechon Out from the Center?

Ultimately then, we are still left with the question with which we began. Was Pope Benedict the Katechon?

As we asked in Chapter One: What if, according to Paul's prophecy, the Restraining force was more than just the Roman Empire, but the union of the Roman Empire and Christ's Church/

---

[191] https://insidethevatican.com/news/newsflash/letter-65-2022-wed-apr-6-vigano/

Stone Kingdom as prophesied by Daniel? As Cardinal Henry Edward Manning writes:

> We have here [2 Thessalonians 2:3-11] a prophecy...of a [spiritual] revolt, which shall precede the second coming of our Lord...The authority, then, from which the revolt is to take place is that of the kingdom of God on earth, prophesied by Daniel [cf. Daniel 2] as the kingdom which the God of heaven should set up...in other words, *the one and universal Church*, founded by our Divine Lord, and spread by His Apostles throughout the world. In this one only kingdom was deposited the true and supernatural pure theism, or knowledge of God, and the true and only faith of God incarnate, with the doctrines and laws of grace. This, then, is the authority from which the revolt is to be made, be that revolt what it may.[192]

> But no one with any discernment can fail to see that it is deeper, mightier, and more widely spread now [1861] more than ever. That this *antichristian power* will one day find its head, and for a time prevail in this world, is certain from prophecy. But this cannot be *until 'he who holdeth shall be taken out of the way...."*[193]

> What, I ask, was the French revolution of 1789, with all its bloodshed, blasphemy, impiety, and cruelty, in all its masquerade of horror and of mockery – what was it but an outbreak of the anti-Christian spirit – the lava font beneath the mountain? And what was the outbreak in 1830 and 1848 but precisely the same principle of Antichrist working

---

[192] Cardinal Henry Edward Manning, *The Present Crisis of the Holy See: A Warning About Antichrist*, (London: Burns and Lambert, 1861), p. 21; https://openlibrary.org/books/OL17957932M/ The_present_crisis_of_the_Holy_See_tested_by_prophecy

[193] Ibid., p. 51.

beneath Christian society, forcing its way upward? In the year 1848 it opened simultaneously [in Revolutions] its many mouths in Berlin, in Vienna, in Turin, in Florence, in Naples, and in Rome itself. In London it heaved and struggled, but its time was not yet. What is all this but the spirit of lawlessness lifting itself against God and man, –the principle of schism, heresy, and infidelity running fused into one mass, and pouring itself forth wherever it can force its way, making craters for its stream wherever the Christian society becomes weak? And this, as it has gone on for centuries, so it will go on until the time shall come *when 'that which holds' shall be taken out of the way'.*"[194]

As we have seen, Aquinas argues similarly in his *Commentary on 2 Thessalonians*:

First comes the revolt...first it is explained as a revolt from the faith because later the faith would be accepted by the whole world...or a revolt of the Roman Empire to which the whole world was subject...but how can this be, since the nations have already withdrawn themselves from the Roman Empire and yet the Antichrist has still not come?

The answer is that it is not over yet but *has changed from a temporal revolt into a spiritual revolt*...And so one should say that the revolt from the Roman Empire should be understood not only as a revolt from the temporal but from *the spiritual empire namely the Catholic faith of the* **Roman Church**. And it is fitting that as Christ came when the

---

[194] Ibid., p. 66.

Roman Empire held sway over all, *so conversely a sign of Antichrist is revolt against it.*[195]

Or again, to quote Manning:

We have now come nearly to a solution of that which I stated in the beginning, namely, how it is that *the power which hinders the revelation of the lawless one is not only a person but a system, and not only a system but a person.* In one word, it is *Christendom and its head;* and therefore, in the person of *the Vicar of Christ, and in that twofold authority* with which, by Divine Providence he has been invested, we see the direct antagonist to the principle of disorder. The lawless one, who knows no law, human or divine, nor obeys any but his own will, has no antagonist on earth more direct than the *Vicar of Jesus Christ...*[196]

[T]he city of Rome will probably become apostate from the Church and Vicar of Jesus Christ; and that Rome will again be punished, for he will depart from it; and the judgment of God will fall on the place from which he once reigned over the nations of the world...*Rome shall apostatize from the faith and drive away the Vicar of Christ...return to its ancient paganism...*[197]

---

[195] St. Thomas Aquinas, *Commentary on the Letters of Saint Paul;* or as he says in his *Commentary on Matthew* 5:13: *"'You are salt.'* Above, the Lord shows the dignity of <u>the Apostles</u> as to the fact that in tribulations they had to be not only patient but also joyful; *but now he speaks of their excellence in so far as they <u>ought to restrain others from evil</u>, and therefore he compares them to salt: you are. And he does two things about this: first, he determines their duty as far as this is concerned, that they keep others from evil; secondly, he shows how they ought to keep themselves from evils,* there: [that if the salt had disappeared]."

[196] Manning, p. 62.

[197] Ibid., p. 104.

St. Paul says that once the Katechon is taken out of the center, an Age of Lawlessness will commence. Did heaven, perhaps, leave us a clue that this was the meaning behind Pope Benedict's "step to the side"? In his *Declaratio*, Benedict stated that "as of February 28th, 2013…the See of Rome, the See of St. Peter will be vacant…" Now Benedict could have chosen any day out of 365 to cease acting as the Bishop of Rome. Could there be any—conscious or unconscious—significance to that date, February 28th, 2013? As it turns out, that very day was the 80th anniversary of Germany's infamous "Reichstag Fire Decree," which suspended constitutional protections and provided the appearance of legality to all subsequent measures enacted by Adolf Hitler's totalitarian Nazi regime! Coincidence?

In the end, in light of all the evidence we have presented of Pope Benedict as Katechon, the following exchange between His Holiness and Peter Seewald in *Last Testament* is intriguing, to say the least:

Peter Seewald: You know the prophecy of Malachy, who in the Middle Ages predicted a list of future popes even to the end of time, at least the end of the Church. According to this list, **the papacy ends after your pontificate.** Is that an issue for you, whether it can actually be that at least you are the last of a series of popes, *as we have known the office so far?*

Pope Benedict: Anything can be…

Appendix I
Collegiality, Synodality and the
Theology Behind Ratzinger's Resignation[198]

"...the very nature of the church [sic] and her mission is at stake. The council fathers described *the church [sic] as a 'pilgrim people,'* a term rooted in Scripture, to develop the image of *the church [sic] previously understood as a perfect society* and a world power to be contended with. As a 'pilgrim people,' the church [sic] is *semper reformanda*, always open to reform and conversion, which is necessary for her to carry out her mission by reading the signs of the times, as Pope John XXIII urged."[199]
Cardinal Blase Cupich, 2022

"Yes, I see that *different church emerging*: a church [sic] that really gets to know herself, because the church [sic] is either synodal or it does not exist."
Cardinal Mario Grech, Secretary General of the Synod on Synodality, 2022

"Collegiality does not agree with Vatican I. Venerable Fathers, beware!"
Bishop Michael Browne at Vatican II

"[Collegiality was] one of the greatest achievements of Vatican II."
Anglican Bishop John Moorman

---

[198] Parts of this chapter are taken from my peer-reviewed journal article: "What Ratzinger Renounced and What is Irrevocable in Pope Emeritus," *Archivio Giuridico di Filippo Serafini*, CLIV, no. 3 (2022), pp. 721-751.
[199] Cardinal Cupich: "Pope Francis' Latin Mass reforms are necessary to secure Vatican II's legacy"; https://www.americamagazine.org/faith/2021/11/10/cupich-traditionis-custodes-latin-mass-241806

"One can best understand Ratzinger by locating him within the movement known as *la nouvelle théologie*."[200] Francis Schüssler Fiorenza, Stillman Professor of Roman Catholic Theological Studies, Harvard Divinity School

Vatican II

As we commemorate the 60th anniversary of the Second Vatican Council, it is worth observing that not a single aspect of the life and practice of the Roman Catholic Church has been left unaffected by it. So it would be naïve in the extreme to think that the 2013 resignation of Pope Benedict XVI was any exception. Indeed, the purpose of this chapter is to elucidate the *"communio"*[201] ecclesiology that underlies Benedict's renunciation: a conspicuously conciliar one, which (as we have examined in detail in Chapter Two) may have, in fact, irreparably undermined it.

Unlike almost every other ecumenical council in Church history, Vatican II (1962-1965) was a "pastoral" council. It formally condemned no errors. It issued no dogmatic decrees demanding adherence to dictums of doctrine under pain of anathema.[202] Indeed, from the very opening of the Council, Pope John XXIII (r.

---

[200] Francis Schüssler Fiorenza; https://bulletin.hds.harvard.edu/from-theologian-to-pope/

[201]https://www.vatican.va/roman_curia/congregations/cfaith/documents/rc_con_cfaith_doc_28051992_communionis-notio_en.html

"Communio was founded in 1972 by [Nouvelle theologians] Hans Urs von Balthasar, Henri de Lubac, and Joseph Ratzinger. It stands for the renewal of theology in continuity with the living Christian tradition, the continuing dialogue of all believers, past and present, 'as if all were simultaneously in the circle;' https://www.communio-icr.com/about

[202] "Vatican II, not being a dogmatic council, did not intend to define any doctrinal truth, limiting itself to indirectly reaffirming—and moreover in an often ambiguous form—doctrines previously defined in a clear and unequivocal way by the infallible authority of the Magisterium. It was unduly and forcibly considered as 'the' Council, the 'superdogma' of the new 'conciliar church', to the point of defining it in relation to that event.

1958-1963) made it clear that there is a difference between the truths of the faith and how those truths are expressed.[203] John hoped that a renewed vocabulary based on just such a distinction would heal the rift with the Eastern Orthodox, the Anglicans, Evangelicals and perhaps, even the unchurched! More than anything else, John wanted a dialogue between the Catholic Church and "Modern Man" unencumbered by stilted language and bygone paradigms.

Collegiality: Dom Lambert Beauduin

Nevertheless, in many ways Vatican II unquestionably *did* take up theological questions of great import and *did* propose

---

[202] (Footnote cont'd) In the conciliar texts there is no explicit mention of what was then done in the liturgical sphere, passing it off as a fulfillment of the Constitution *Sacrosanctum Concilium*. On the other hand, there are many critical aspects of the so-called 'reform', which represents a betrayal of the will of the Council Fathers and of the pre-conciliar liturgical heritage." Carlo Vigano, "The Thread on which the Council Hangs," January 21, 2023; https://www.stilumcuriae.com/il-filo-a-cui-e-appeso-il-concilio-mons-vigano; "The Second Vatican Council has not been treated as a part of the entire living Tradition of the Church, but as an end of Tradition, a new start from zero. *The truth is that this particular council defined no dogma at all*, and deliberately chose to remain on a modest level, as a merely pastoral council; and yet many treat it as though it had made itself into a sort of superdogma which takes away the importance of all the rest." Joseph Ratzinger, July 13, 1988, Santiago, Chile; *The Wanderer*, (June 22, 2000); https://www.catholicculture.org/culture/library/view.cfm?recnum=3032

[203] "What is needed is that this certain and immutable doctrine, to which the faithful owe obedience, be studied afresh and reformulated in contemporary terms. For this deposit of faith, or truths which are contained in our time-honored teaching is one thing; the manner in which these truths are set forth (with their meaning preserved intact) is something else...We must work out ways and means of expounding these truths in a manner more consistent with a predominantly pastoral view of the Church's teaching office...the Lord's truth is indeed eternal. Human ideologies change. Successive generations give rise to varying errors, and these often vanish as quickly as they came, like mist before the sun.

The Church has always opposed these errors, and often condemned them with the utmost severity. Today, however, Christ's Bride prefers the balm of mercy to the arm of severity. She believes that present needs are best served by explaining more fully the purport of her doctrines, rather than by publishing condemnations." Pope John XIII, "Opening Address to Second Vatican Council," October 11, 1962.

143

definitive solutions, *just as if it were a dogmatic council.* [204] Among these, there can be no greater example than the complete reinterpretation of the Church's understanding of "Church":

those in favor of *collegiality* argued that the doctrine of Papal Primacy as taught at Vatican I needed to be "balanced" by the principle of collegiality in governance. *The essential doctrine of collegiality is that the power of jurisdiction [power to govern] had been entrusted, not to Peter alone, but to "the Twelve"*; while not denying that Peter had the primacy, the innovators suggested that it was *by virtue of his presidency of the apostolic college* that Peter held this rank, not by the special, direct commission of Christ. Authority is entrusted to the Twelve, and Peter has authority by virtue of being head of the Twelve. *Thus the Twelve is the true body of authority. This is the heart of collegiality.*[205]

In the first half of the twentieth century, literally only a handful of people within the Church were conversant with "collegiality." One hundred years later, however, the Vatican is

---

[204] "[The Council's] task is to bring certain troublesome theological controversies to a close...Its task is to finally manifest to the faithful of the Catholic Church and to our brothers and sisters from separated communities what is the true concept of the orders of the sacred hierarchy, of which it was said, "The Holy Spirit has set up overseers [*episcopos*] to govern the Church of God" (Acts 20:28), and indeed with a firm authority [*cum auctoritate certa*] *which may not be called into doubt."* Pope Paul VI, *"Allocutio: In signo Sanctae Crucis* (September 14, 1964)," *Acta Apostolica Sedis* 56, no. 13 (Oct. 24, 1964), pp. 805-816, at 809; Citation and translation by Lawrence J. King, *The Authoritative Weight of Non-Definitive Magisterial Teaching*, (2016), p.106.

[205] Phillip Campbell, "Collegiality: The Church's Pandora's Box," *Unam Sanctam Catholicam*, (February 9, 2014); http://unamsanctamcatholicam.com/2022/09/collegiality-the-churchs-pandoras-box

now proudly hosting the great "Synod on Synodality"[206]—and proudly boasting of the participation not only of Catholic bishops, but of men (*and women*), *even from non-Christian religions!*[207]

From its cradle, collegiality was a term first nursed by an obscure Belgian monk, Dom Lambert Beauduin, O.S.B. (1873–1960). Beauduin was a man utterly enamored with "ecumenism," the process of using dialogue for removing obstacles preventing Catholic reunification with the non-Catholic "separated communities." It was a passion Beauduin shared with his friend—none other than Pope John XXIII, back when he was still papal nuncio, Angelo Roncalli. Here is the testimony of the abbot of Beauduin's monastery:

> In 1958, [Abbot] Fr. Roger Poelman found himself one day in Chevetogne, in Fr. Beauduin's room. The two engaged in a crude dialogue about the ailing Pius XII.

---

[206] "The Synod on Synodality, launched by Pope Francis in 2021, is a multi-year process that involves gathering opinions of lay Catholics – and even non-Catholics – in every diocese in the world ahead of the Synod of Bishops in Rome next October [2023]. Pope Francis has described the goal of the Synod as creating 'a different Church,' and top synodal officials have indicated that it could lead to changes in Church doctrine and leadership.

The relator general of the Synod, Cardinal Jean-Claude Hollerich, sparked outrage and accusations of heresy earlier this year for claiming that Catholic teaching on the sinfulness of homosexual acts is 'no longer correct' and needs 'revision.' National synodal reports from multiple Western countries have also highlighted calls for doctrinal change, including on homosexuality and the ordination of women, and the official Vatican website for the Synod has repeatedly infuriated Catholics by promoting homosexual relationships and dissident activist groups;" https://www.lifesitenews.com/news/cardinal-mueller-says-pope-francis-synod-is-a-hostile-takeover-of-the-church-in-explosive-interview/?utm_source=top_news&utm_campaign=usa

[207] "'in our country [Malta], we have a large community of Muslims, but a group of them call themselves 'Christ,' and so the conference invited them to participate. Cardinal Mario Grech [Secretary General of the Synod] remarked, 'They admire Jesus so much that *although they are Muslims*, they have this interest in Jesus, *so what should keep us from listening to them as well?*';" Gerard O'Connell, "Exclusive: Cardinal Grech on drafting the first global synod synthesis—and what's in store for phase 2," *America* (September 21, 2022); https://www.americamagazine.org/faith/2022/09/21/cardinal-mario-grech-synod-synodality-243827

Beauduin: "I warn you: he will die very soon. And his steward will be Roncalli!"

Poelman: "That nuncio from Paris?"

Beauduin: "Well, yes! You'll see. He'll announce the Council and he'll do it from an ecumenical perspective."

On October 28, 1958, on the occasion of the priestly ordination in Chevetogne, there is a bonfire meeting; it is the second day of the conclave. Fr. Beauduin repeats like a mantra: "Roncalli will become pope and declare an ecumenical council."[208]

Astoundingly, Beauduin not only accurately predicts that the cardinals will elect Roncalli, but he also prophesies correctly that Roncalli will call a Council—a council whose principal aim is ecumenism!

This was no coincidence. According to one of the most prominent of the Council Fathers, Vatican II was itself the brainchild, not only of Roncalli, but of Beauduin:

In a letter to Vatican scholar G. Alberigo [a "Bologna School" Modernist] dated March 19, 1985, Cardinal

---

[208] The conversation with Poelman was recorded twice: on May 18, 1994, and on December 13, 1996. Loonbeek Mortoau, *Un pionnier Dom Lambert Beauduin...*, p. 1467. My translation from the Polish; as cited in Artur A. Kasprzak Odnowa, "The Episcopate's Revival of Theology as the Beginning of the Collegiality Doctrine in the Analysis of the Development of Theology and Events in the Belgian Church Before the Second Vatican Council," *Roczniki Teologiczne* LXI, 2 (2014), pp. 135-178; 173, nt. 175.

Suenens[209] [(1904-1996), infamous arch-modernist Primate of Belgium] wrote: "I understand that you are anxious to find an answer to the question of how Pope John XXIII came to think of convening the Council. Probably many factors had an influence—not to omit the inspiration of the Holy Spirit! [sic]—*but I believe that Fr. Lambert Beauduin played an important role.* When Cardinal Roncalli—the future Pope—was an apostolic delegate in Istanbul, he held talks on the subject. *Beauduin argued at length with him about the need to* **balance Vatican Council I** after the promulgation of a new Council that would work out additions to unfinished questions.[210]

Just who was this Fr. Beauduin, who played such an "important role" in influencing Pope John to call Vatican II?

After his ordination in 1897, Beauduin joined the *Congregation des Aumôniers du Travail,* a society of "worker-priests" established by the Bishop of Liège, Mgr. Victor Doutreloux. He then spent seven years living among the workers in the footsteps of Fr. Pottier, a political agitator silenced by Pope Leo XIII:

---

[209] Ibid., p. 173; "Leo Jozef Suenens…one of the most important prelates at the Council, argued that to find the true meaning of a conciliar document one has to identify the 'underlying thought of the majority,' which is often concealed by the final language of the documents. As a result of compromises designed to achieve unanimity, '*the texts are sometimes far richer in what they imply than in what they affirm.*' [sic!] In the future, '*it will be the task of men moved by the Holy Spirit to draw out all the vital riches contained in the conciliar texts – and, for that matter, in all that was said both inside and outside the Council hall, but which has become an integral part of Vatican II.*'" Leo Jozef Suenens (as Léon-Joseph Suenens), "Introduction: Co-Responsibility: Dominating Idea of the Council and its Pastoral Consequences," in *Theology of Renewal, vol. 2: Renewal of Religious Structures: Proceedings of the Congress on the Theology of the Renewal of the Church; Centenary of Canada, 1867-1967,* ed. L. K. Shook (New York, NY: Herder and Herder, 1968), pp. 7-18, at pp. 10-11. As cited, Lawrence King, p. 141.

[210] Ibid; FConc. Suenens, no. 2867.

The experience radicalized his outlook. Just as he saw society in terms of a conflict between the rich and the poor, industrialists and workers, he saw a counterpart in the constitution of the Church. He argued that active participation in the liturgy would unite the faithful for social change and for the "emancipation" of the laity from "domination" by the clergy. At this point the Liturgical Movement was effectively turned into a platform for Marxist propaganda within the Church...[211]

In 1906, Beauduin joined the Benedictine Abbey of Mont César in Leuven, Belgium. The movement for the "renewal" of the liturgy which produced *Sacrosanctum Concilium* and the *Novus Ordo Missae* can ultimately be traced back there:[212]

Mont César was to become the nexus of strategic planning for various projects: promoting "active participation" among the laity, adapting the liturgy to contemporary needs, linking it to social activism, reorienting monastic life (in Beauduin's opinion, "too closed in upon itself") towards the world outside the cloister, and fostering ecumenism among religions without seeking conversion to Catholicism...

---

[211] Carol Byrne, "The Start of the New Liturgical Reform" https://www.traditioninaction.org/HotTopics/f075_Dialogue_3.htm

[212] Carol Byrne, "Active Participation: *Actuosa* and Subverting the Law of Prayer," *One Peter Five*, https://OnePeterFive.com/actuosa-subverting/
"Let us consider an intriguing dilemma that has occupied the minds of all involved in the Liturgical Movement since its beginning: the novel principle of active participation (*participatio actuosa*), which Vatican II's Constitution on the Liturgy promoted as 'the aim to be achieved before all else.' It all started with Dom Lambert Beauduin's accusation that the faithful were 'dumb and idle spectators' who needed to be aroused from their 'torpor' and made to engage actively in the liturgy. That was the first false assumption on which the requirement for active participation was based. But Catholics had for centuries already been participating *fully* in the Mass with great spiritual benefit through silent prayer and meditation on the Holy Sacrifice. It was a method that produced countless saints and bore fruit in plentiful vocations to the priesthood."

Beauduin naturally presented his theories in the form of a binary opposition between priests and laity, as a result of which there could be two – and only two – possible outcomes: the total domination of one side by the other. The polarized context of this message apes the standard Marxist outlook by implying that "ownership" of the liturgy was "in the hands of the few" and that the "oppressed masses" should take back what rightfully belongs to them by virtue of their Baptism.[213]

In 1925, Beauduin delivered a lecture, *L'église anglicane unie, mais non absorbée* in which he argued that the Church of England should be "reunited" with—not simply "absorbed" by—the Roman Church. In that same year, he founded the monastery of Chevetogne devoted to ecumenical efforts at Christian unity. His speech occurred within the context of the "Malines Conversations," held in Mechelen (Malines), Belgium from 1921 to 1926. These were informal dialogues between:

> a select group of Catholic and Anglican theologians. The conversations have their origins on the chance meeting and subsequent friendship of Charles Lindley Wood, the second Viscount of Halifax, and Abbé Fernand Portal, a French Lazarist priest. The 1920 Lambeth Conference's Appeal to Unity provided an opportunity for Lord Halifax to approach the Archbishop of Brussels, Cardinal Désiré Joseph Mercier, who was already engaged with the question of unity.[214]

Though the exact content of these talks is not entirely known, the Catholic hierarchy of England protested that the

[213] Byrne, https://www.traditioninaction.org/HotTopics/f075_Dialogue_3.htm

[214] http://www.christianunity.va/content/unitacristiani/en/news/2021/2021-06-14-malines-conversations.html

nature of the unity Beauduin envisioned was contrary to the principles of the papal encyclical, *Apostolicae Curae*. Pius XI officially put a stop to the talks and in 1928, issued the encyclical *Mortalium Animos: On Fostering True Religious Unity* in which he condemned Catholic participation in Protestant ecumenical projects.

As for Beauduin's activism, it resulted in his being transferred to En Calcat Abbey in Dourgne, in 1932 where he remained exiled until 1951. But like almost all Modernist innovators, he was initially subject to sanction only to return later in the tow of a novel and more "progressive" pontificate.

Belgian innovation in liturgy and ecumenism, therefore, is the original source for Vatican II's novel concept of "collegiality." None other than Joseph Ratzinger, himself, affirms this:

> The notion of episcopal collegiality, which likewise numbers among the main pillars of the ecclesiology of the Second Vatican Council is most intimately connected with Eucharistic ecclesiology...If I am not mistaken, the first one to formulate it clearly and thereby open the door for the Council on this point was the Belgian liturgical scholar, Bernard Botte [younger contemporary of Beauduin]...In the treatment of the idea of collegiality, the catchword has been mentioned...Church as People of God. What does it mean?...the concept of the People of God was introduced to the Council above all as an ecumenical bridge...the rediscovery of the Church [sic] after World War I was a thoroughly Catholic and Protestant phenomena; even the liturgical renewal was in no way limited to the Catholic Church.[215]

---

[215] Joseph Ratzinger, "The Ecclesiology of the Second Vatican Council," *Communio*, vol. 13, no.3 (1986).

Collegiality: Yves Congar

The next pioneer of "collegiality" with connections to the Belgian movement is the Modernist theologian, Yves Congar. He was ordained a priest in 1930 and the following year, chose as the topic for his lectoral thesis, "The Unity of the Church." The year after that he met Beauduin:

> Fr. Congar established relations with Dom Beauduin and Fr. Couturier, being inspired by the latter with an "evolutionist" notion of the Church. He began to frequent the Monastery of Chevetogne and the 'Ecumenical Days' held there during the 1940's and 1950's.[216] The Catholic Ecumenists of these years were intent to extend the concept of Mystical Body to all the Christian "churches," understanding it in a "pneumatic" sense *that prescinded from its juridical, institutional structure.* Fr. Congar also came under the influence of Fr. Johann-Adam Moehler who inspired him in his turn with the doctrine of a Church 'the whole of whose Constitution is nothing other than Love Incarnate.'[217]

As Philip Campbell explains:

> We have seen that the origin of the phrase was based in the ecumenical work of Dom Beauduin and Fr. Congar. Moving forward to Vatican II, ecumenism was one of the main arguments offered in favor of collegiality. Since the primacy of the pope was a stumbling block to ecumenical

---

[216] "Indeed, numerous Belgian theologians who took part in the ecumenical sessions at Chevetogne also became 'actors' at the Council. They were involved as bishops, members of commissions, or as official consultants to the bishops on theological matters, the so-called *periti*. Among them were such personalities as: 'Monsignor Charue, G. Philips, J. Dupont, Ch. Moeller and G. Thils." Odnowa, p. 157.

[217] https://rorate-caeli.blogspot.com/2021/05/the-council-and-eclipse-of-god-part-x.html#more

dialogue, it was necessary to minimize its importance by highlighting the "collegial" nature to the Church's government. If it could be shown that the bishops around the world retained a power to govern collectively as a "college", Catholicism would be more palatable to non-Catholics who objected to the primacy of Peter. Besides Fr. Congar, then a *peritus* at the Council, the other major proponent of collegiality was Bishop Charue of Namur, vice-president of the Theological Commission. Charue's talking points were taken from the book *The Primacy of Peter* (1960), a book authored by Chevetogne monk Oliver Rousseau in which the "juridical" notion of "power" was contrasted with a more "collegial" ecclesiology based on "love." As we can see, a dangerous dualism was being introduced into the ecclesiological thinking of the Council Fathers—a Church of the "spirit" opposed to a rigidly inflexible hierarchy.[218]

Robert Nugent, speaking of the inflexible hierarchy of Pope Pius XII and its treatment of Congar writes:

The 'Holy Office' in practice rules the church and makes everyone bow down to it through fear or through interventions. It is the supreme Gestapo, unyielding, whose decisions cannot be discussed.[219]

Congar was banished from France to Oxford in 1955, where he was forbidden to engage in any public talks, writings or other interactions with non-Catholics. But in time, Vatican II vindicated Congar, as well as the others who were censured by the Vatican officials during the final years of

---

[218] Campbell, "Collegiality."

[219] Robert Nugent, *Silence Speaks*, (New York, NY/Mahwah, NJ: Paulist Press, 2011).

Pius's pontificate: Henry de Lubac and Karl Rahner in particular.[220]

Collegiality Against Primacy

As for collegiality and the Council:

The major debates on collegiality in the schema that would become *Lumen Gentium* occurred in October 1963. The progressives, led by Cardinals Meyer, Leger, König, Alfrink and De Smedt, argued in favor of collegiality, *and* for the establishment of permanent national episcopal conferences, which were held to be the appropriate structural expression of collegiality. The theory was bitterly contested by Cardinals Siri, Ruffini and Archbishops Staffa and Sigaud.

Archbishop Sigaud, for example, stated that the schema gave the impression that new doctrine was being taught. He also stated that he believed that collegiality would imply that the Church would be ruled "by means of a sort of permanent council."[221] Archbishop Lefebvre also argued that the authority of episcopal conference would not only weaken papal authority, but the authority of individual bishops...

When certain members of the Theological Commission proposed adding clear explanations of the teaching of Vatican I to the schema to highlight the continuity with the

---

[220] https://www.forbes.com/sites/johnfarrell/2014/08/11/the-cautious-pope-and-the-evolution-encyclical/?sh=6f615d84572d

[221] Archbishop Proença Sigaud, interview with *Divine Word Service* (October 10, 1963), in Campbell.

doctrine of papal primacy, their move was blocked by
Rahner and Ratzinger.[222]

Collegiality: Order vs Jurisdiction

As one of the principal actors of the Second Vatican
Council,[223] Ratzinger is acutely responsible for a major paradigm
shift in the understanding of "Church." As he reflected just after
the close of the Council: "Vatican II tried to...formulate a
genuinely spiritual view of the episcopate as a complement to
papal primacy. The Church was no longer seen in terms of
political models [i.e. power], but in terms of biblical images...the
Church is neither a parliamentary nor *monarchical* super-
state..."[224]

In another book written shortly after the Council, Ratzinger
argues that Vatican II has finally righted a major wrong in the
Church's understanding of Sacred Power. He argues that the
Power of Order, whereby bishops (and priests) receive irrevocable
sacramental powers, and the Power of Jurisdiction, whereby
bishops receive authority to govern the Church, must no longer be
viewed as *distinct* phenomena; otherwise there can never be
genuine *collegiality*:

If the proposed distinction [Order vs. Jurisdiction] were
undoubtedly right, the following argument would be
logical: the power of order refers only to sacramental
action, and thus specifically to the Eucharistic event. This

---

[222] The episode is related in the biography of Msgr. Michele Maccarrone, who
was on the Commission. De Mattei, p. 317; Campbell.

[223] First as personal advisor to Cardinal Frings, Archbishop of Cologne and
then a month later, he was named an official *peritus* of the Council.

[224] Joseph Ratzinger, *Theological Highlights of Vatican II*, (New York, NY /
Mahwah, NJ: Paulist Press, 1966), p. 128. In contrast, Pope St. Pius X referred to the
Church as: "a sovereignty of one person, that is a monarchy," Apostolic Letter *Ex
Quo*; Denz. 2147a.

has nothing to do with "collegiality," the priest's liturgical *actio* in the Mass is rather something he alone must perform *hic et nunc*. The power of jurisdiction refers, it is true, to the church, but only the pope has jurisdiction over the whole church. *Every other bishop receives jurisdiction only for a delimited particular church, in which then (apart from the pope) he alone is competent. Therefore, even the power of jurisdiction is not to be understood collegially.* Thus—and this would be the concluding consequence of the whole argument— collegiality is not conjoined with the essential functions of the episcopal office and at most is a moral postulate in the fortuitous relations of bishops to each other.[225]

Before the advent of collegiality, "being bishop" was seen as strictly an "office of local jurisdiction"—jurisdiction that came from the Pope. This is how the draft Constitution on the Church planned for the Council phrased it:

As for the constitution of this august College, all residential Bishops living in peace with the Apostolic See are by their own right members of it, and no Bishop, whether residential or not, can belong to this College unless by direct act or by tacit consent he is admitted into it by the

---

[225] Joseph Ratzinger, *Nuovo Populo Di Dio*, (Brescia: Editrice Queriniana, 1971), p. 238; My translation from the Italian: "Se la distinzione proposta fosse senz'altro giusta, sarrebe logica la seguente argomentazione: il potere di ordine si riferisce soltanto all'azione sacramentale, e quindi in particolare al fatto eucaristico. Cio non ha nulla a che fare con la "collegialita", la actio liturgica del sacerdote nella messa e piuttosto qualcosa che egli solo deve compiere *hic et nunc*. Il potere di giurisdizione si riferisce, e vero, alla chiesa, ma soltanto il papa ha giurisdizione su tutta la chiesa. Ogni altro vescovo riceve giurisdizione soltanto per una chiesa particolare delimitata, nella quale allora (oltre il papa) egli solo e competante. Percio anche il potere di giurisdizione non e da intendersi collegialmente. Quindi -- e questa sarebbe la conseguenza conclusiva di tutto l'argomento -- la collegialita non e congiunta con le funzioni essenziali dell'ufficio episcopale ed al massimo e un postulato morale nei rapporti fortuiti dei vescovi tra loro."

155

successor of Peter, the Vicar of Christ, and Head of the College.[226]

Although Ratzinger is loath to admit it, when the Council rejected this wording, it raised the profile of the bishops at the expense of traditional papal sovereignty:

[In the original 1962 draft cited above] Membership of the college of bishops [*communio hierarchica*] could only be residential bishops...the requirement for membership was jurisdiction over a particular diocese, [jurisdiction] conferred by the pope [known as *missio canonica*]...the college would appear in the long run to be nothing more than an institution of papal privilege and the great idea of collegiality threatened to evaporate [sic]...[227]

But for Ratzinger, *Lumen Gentium* "thankfully" replaced the 1962 draft schema. Here are the pertinent selections (articles 21 and 22) from Chapter 3:

21. ...by Episcopal consecration the fullness of the sacrament of Orders is conferred, that fullness of power namely, which both in the Church's liturgical practice and in the language of the Fathers of the Church is called the high priesthood, the supreme power of the sacred ministry But *Episcopal consecration, together with the office [munus] of sanctifying, also confers the office [munera] of teaching and of governing, which, however, of its very nature, can be exercised only in hierarchical communion with the head and the members of the college*...Therefore it pertains to the bishops to admit newly elected members into the Episcopal body by means of the sacrament of Orders.

---

[226] "Draft of a Dogmatic Constitution," Chapter 4.
[227] Ibid., p. 126.

22. Just as in the Gospel, the Lord so disposing, St. Peter and the other apostles constitute one apostolic college, so in a similar way the Roman Pontiff, the successor of Peter, and the bishops, the successors of the apostles, are joined together...*one is constituted a member of the Episcopal body in virtue of sacramental consecration* and hierarchical communion with the head and members of the body.

...the Roman Pontiff has full, supreme, and universal power over the Church. And he is always free to exercise this power. The order of bishops, which succeeds to the college of apostles and gives this apostolic body continued existence, is also the subject of supreme and full power over the universal Church, provided we understand this body together with its head the Roman Pontiff and never without this head. This power can be exercised only with the consent of the Roman Pontiff.[228]

The Council fathers were asked to vote on October 29th and 30th, 1963:

Does it please the fathers that the Council should affirm:

(1) That episcopal consecration is the highest degree of the sacrament of Holy Orders.[229]

---

[228] *Lumen gentium*; https://www.vatican.va/archive/hist_councils/ii_vatican_council/documents/vat-ii_const_19641121_lumen-gentium_en.html

[229] "...the fact that the episcopal consecration confers the power of sanctifying is nothing new. As for calling it a sacrament, while *Lumen Gentium* does decide upon a question that was freely disputed by theologians, it is in keeping on this point with the opinion of the majority of the Conciliar Fathers [the vote on question #1 was 2,123 to 34] and was already strongly implied by Pope Pius XII in the Apostolic Constitution *Sacramentum Ordinis* on November 30, 1947;" Fr. Nicolas Cadiet, "A Study of Collegiality at the Second Vatican Council," October 29, 2018; https://sspx.org/en/news-events/news/study-collegiality-second-vatican-council-41649

(2) That each bishop who is legitimately *consecrated* in communion with the bishops and the pope, their head and principle of unity, *becomes a member of the Episcopal College.*

(3) That this Body or College of Bishops succeeds the College of the Apostles in the mission of evangelizing, sanctifying and governing, and that *this College of Bishops*, united with its head, the Roman Pontiff and never without this head-it being understood that the primatial right of head remains whole and entire-*possesses a supreme and plenary authority in the universal Church.*

(4) That this power belongs, *by divine right*, to the *Episcopal College* united with its head.

(5) That the revival of the diaconate as a distinct and permanent grade of the sacred ministry is opportune.

The questions were approved by a solid (though not unanimous) margin, around 75% overall. The key question here is question three, because it introduces a legal entity unknown in the entire history of the Church—the Episcopal College as a whole, which is attributed "supreme and plenary authority."[230]

Collegiality: Episcopacy Against the Papacy

Congar, referencing the Communist takeover of Russia in 1917, characterized this vote as *"the Church's October Revolution."*[231] He is also notorious for saying: "For a thousand years everything

---

[230] Campbell, "Collegiality."
[231] https://sspx.org/en/collegiality-error-vatican-ii-2

among us has been seen and constructed from the papal angle, not from that of the episcopate and its collegiality. Now THIS history, THIS theology, THIS canon law needs to be done."[232] (emphasis original)

As Julia Meloni writes of Congar:

his "half-way" revolution generated Vatican II's "ambivalent" and ambiguous documents. For instance, after Rahner and others attacked the original schema on collegiality, some counter-revolutionaries warned Pope Paul VI that the new schema's ambiguous passages could, after the council, be interpreted in a radical way. As Fr. Ralph Wiltgen explains, collegiality, in its extreme form, stipulated that the pope "would be bound in conscience to request the opinion of the college of bishops before making a pronouncement." Ultimately, says Wiltgen, "one of the extreme liberals made the mistake of referring, in writing, to some of these ambiguous passages, and indicating how they would be interpreted after the Council." Paul VI wept at the revolutionaries' deception. He announced that a preliminary note would rule out a liberal interpretation of the council's text. But according to de Mattei, the note was a precarious "compromise"—ambivalently placing papal primacy and episcopal collegiality on the same level.[233]

Here is how a journalist from the (notoriously left-wing) *National Catholic Reporter* described the situation on the eve of the adoption of *Lumen Gentium*:

---

[232] Yves Congar, *Journal*, Sept. 25, 1964, quoted in Roberto de Mattei, *The Second Vatican Council: An Unwritten Story*, (Fitzwilliam, NH: Loreto Publications, 2012), pp. 313-314. Or as he taught less hyperbolically: "Rome is the center of ecclesial communion, but not its source."

[233] Julia Meloni, *The St. Gallen Mafia: Exposing the Secret Reformist Group Within the Church*, (TAN Books, 2021); Rev Ralph Wiltgen, *Rhine Flows Into the Tiber*, (Devon: Augustine Publishing Company, 1978), pp. 228-232.

Other Issues have taken the headlines at the moment, but *collegiality is still the key to the significance of the Second Vatican Council.* The debate on birth control, the schema on ecumenism, the declaration on religious liberty—these and others are of deep and lasting importance, *but the practical implementation of collegiality will have much to do with the effective communication of council decisions on these matters to the faithful, and with their administration and interpretation in decades and centuries to come.* Collegiality put into practice almost inevitably means a more open and more flexible Church, since by its nature it means bringing the varied experiences and outlooks of all the world's bishops—and their priests and people—into play in shaping the Church's response to the times. It is not surprising, then, that those who administered the pre-council Church should resist the idea of collegiality and seek to diminish its practical import.

... Archbishop Staffa made use of a visit to the U.S. to enlist the sympathies of Cardinal Cushing. Instead of the usual juridical objections, Staffa painted a dramatic picture of a Church which, *because of collegiality, could be split by opposition of bishops to the pope.* Archbishop Staffa returned to Rome confident that he had won a recruit, and that Cardinal Cushing would persuade other U.S. bishops to oppose collegiality. No sooner did the Boston cardinal arrive at the council for the third session, however, than others convinced him that his much-loved Pope John had been a proponent of collegiality, and that he would have been disappointed if his American friend allied himself with those who had always opposed the council. But the most damaging blow to the conservatives: the partial defection of archbishop Pietro Parente, who once was regarded as the right-hand man of Cardinal Alfredo Ottaviani, considered leader of the conservatives.

Archbishop Parente not only presented the statement on collegiality to the council, but clashed with the canonists and jurists who attacked it. Parente recommended the text on collegiality as integrating the theological concepts of St. Paul and St. Augustine with the juridical concept of the Church elaborated in the 11th century.

... Archbishop Staffa addressed a meeting of the 480 Italian bishops convoked during this third session in an attempt to solidify Italian opposition to collegiality. But when the council votes on collegiality were taken, the highest "no" vote was 323, showing that in this case the Italian vote must have been far from solidly conservative.[234]

---

[234] Desmond O'Grady, "Collegiality: the crucial issue to 'the old firm' at the Vatican," *National Catholic Reporter*, vol. 1, no. 3 (November 11, 1964), p.3; https://thecatholicnewsarchive.org/?a=d&d=ncr19641111-01.2.18&srpos=60&e=-------en-20--1--txt-txIN--------

"...it would seem that nothing stands in the way of a full implementation of collegiality in the central government of the Church. But this is not the case. For one thing, Pope Paul has yet to act. For another, the conservatives are still capable of audacious moves to balk the will of the majority of council Fathers. The attempt to ensure the rewriting of the Jewish and religious liberty declarations by those opposed to them is patent proof of this. Perhaps the most serious majority worry is that as post-conciliar commissions are established to carry out the will of the council, they may run up against a series of parallel institutions in the Church's central bureaucracy. Such a clash has already occurred between the post-conciliar liturgy commission and the Congregation of Rites over competence and interpretation of the conciliar decree on the liturgy. It has raised the possibility of discord and confusion in the post-conciliar period when conservative forces will make full use of their experience. Even a senate of bishops would be weakened by one current opinion among some who support the principle of collegiality, but say it applies only to the bishops as a whole, not to a select senate of bishops. In any case, a senate meeting for two months a year would leave the curia in command for the other ten. It is to be hoped that Pope Paul can see the way for reorganization of the central government of the Church which reflects the new realities revealed by the council. In a situation where pre-conciliar and post-conciliar structures duplicate and flank one another like stratifications of Church history, there is every advantage for the old firm."

Bishops Rule the *Universal* Church Too?

In the end, the teaching of *Lumen Gentium* 22 that *"...one is constituted a member of the Episcopal body in virtue of sacramental consecration"* remained unaltered, the linchpin in the Progressive takeover of the Church. As Ratzinger remarks:

> This passage also breaches the wall that separated the Middle Ages from the early Church, and hence the Latin West from the Churches of the East [i.e. the Orthodox]. We see the reason why future references to Peter Lombard, Albert, Bonaventure, and Thomas Aquinas will no longer be meaningful in this issue. [sic!]

> This passage consists in the inconspicuous little statement that membership in the college of bishops is attained through sacramental ordination and communion with the head and members of the college. This statement gives episcopal collegiality a double basis but in such a way that these two roots are inseparably connected...

> *...collegiality is not based on a papally conferred jurisdiction*, paralleling the sacrament of ordination as though that sacrament were merely an individual gift rather, collegiality reaches into the very essence of the sacrament, which carries within it an intrinsic correlation to the community of bishops...

Or as Richard DeClue writes in an article for *Communio* in which he quotes Ratzinger, its founder:

> In the postapostolic age, however, the bishops took on the universal office as an addition to their local office [as Ratzinger writes in *Called to Communion*:]*"They now assumed a responsibility whose scope transcended the*

local principle." This newly acquired role of the bishops ensured that the missionary mandate given to the apostles to preach to all nations did not end with the death of the last apostle. *Thus, bishops now have concern, not only for their own local Churches, but also for the Church as a whole spread throughout the world.*[235]

But aren't these errors?

To start with, Bishop Gasser claimed that *dogmatic council Vatican I taught*: *"The bishops succeeded the Apostles not as succeeding to a universal apostolate* but rather to an episcopate as rulers of individual churches."*[236]

Furthermore, these contrarian positions of Ratzinger and the other progressive Council Fathers seem eerily reminiscent of the errors of Johann Valentin Eybel (1741-1805), an Austrian canon law professor excommunicated for spreading falsity regarding Church and papacy. In 1782, Eybel authored (anonymously) the booklet, *What is the Pope?* [*Was ist der Papst?*] on the occasion of Pope Pius VI's (r. 1775-1799) visit to Vienna. In it, he denied the traditional Catholic teaching on the papacy and promoted Febronianism. In response, Pius VI released the encyclical, *Super Soliditate* on November 28, 1786.[237] In it, Pius condemns Eybel's teaching that

> *every bishop is called by God as much as the Pope is, to the government of the Church, and that he has received no less power*; that Jesus Christ gave the same power to all the Apostles; that *what some men believe can be obtained only*

---

[235] Richard DeClue, "Primacy and Collegiality in the Works of Joseph Ratzinger," *Communio*, vol. 35, no. 4 (2008), pp. 642–670; 652.

[236] Vincent Gasser, *Official Relatio*, 007; https://sites.google.com/site/thetaboriclight/documents/document-05-official-relatio-of-vatican-i

[237] https://novusordowatch.org/pius6-bull-super-soliditate/

from the Sovereign Pontiff, and granted only by him, in so far as it depends upon consecration and ecclesiastical jurisdiction, can be obtained equally from every bishop; [238]

And Pius continues:

Eybel has not feared to stigmatize as *fanatic* those whom he has heard cry out at the sight of the Pope: "This is he who has received from God the keys of the kingdom of heaven with power to bind and loose! This is he to whom no other bishop can be compared! *This is he from whom the bishops themselves receive their authority as he has received from God the supreme authority!* This is the Vicar of Jesus Christ, the visible Head of the Church, the Supreme Judge of the Faithful! Is it therefore fanatic — We say this only with horror — is that word therefore fanatic of Jesus Christ, which promises to Peter, with the power of binding and loosing, the keys of the Kingdom of Heaven, those keys which St. Optatus of Mila did not hesitate — following Tertullian — to say *had been put into the hands of St. Peter alone to be handed on to others?* (Tertullian, Scorp., XI; Optatus of Mila, ibid.)[239]

Five years following the conclusion of the Council, Bishop Remi De Roo (r. 1962-1999), the longest serving bishop in Canadian history, writes in Eybel-like fashion about

the rediscovery at the Second Vatican Council of our common baptismal priesthood. From parishioner to pope we are brothers in Christ. *This basic relationship is primary, more important than any other. No office or function in the Church can override this fundamental*

---

[238] Pope Pius VI, *Super Soliditate*, Denz. 1500.
[239] Ibid.

relationship. Through Christ, the "first born of the Father," we have all become "sons in the Son." The Pastoral Constitution on The Church in the Modern World recalls this doctrine of universal brotherhood...[240]

Was this not condemned by Pius VI?

1515 15. The doctrine which proposes that the Church "must be considered as one mystical body composed of Christ, the head, and the faithful, who are its members through an ineffable union, by which in a marvelous way we become with Him one sole priest, one sole victim, one sole perfect adorer of God the Father, in spirit and in truth," *understood in this sense, that no one belongs to the body of the Church except the faithful,* [i.e. there is no ontological distinction between Pope and bishops, clergy and laity] who are perfect adorers in spirit and in truth **is heretical**.[241]

And De Roo (who died at age 97 in 2022) fantasizes further:

*One can only hope this trend develops into a **full collegial process** of policy and decision making. Is it too much to dream of the day when in the midst of vigorous local churches, **the Petrine***

---

[240] Bishop Remi De Roo, "Collegiality and the Petrine Office in the Pastoral Work of the Church," CTSA Proceedings, 25 (1970); "The major shifts which occurred during the Council did not come without pain and travail. Divergent perspectives on substantial issues brought about fierce clashes. At times there was emotional reaction to some of the developments. As one example, I well remember the impassioned declaration of Cardinal Ottaviani during one of the debates around collegiality. He interrupted his fluent Latin to shout in his native Italian, *'Il Papa parla da solo!'* the Pope speaks alone!...

[240 (footnote cont'd)] The leader of the Vatican Curia, like some other Vatican officials, perhaps felt threatened at the thought of taking any guidance whatsoever from a proposed College of Bishops. I have since come to realize that intelligent people can unconsciously remain slaves to defunct theories when they do not know the source of the ideas they hold as traditional and beyond questioning;" https://vatican2voice.org/92symp/deroo.htm

[241] *Auctorem Fidei*, Denz. 1515.

office will function more like a coordinative force than an imperial one? The pope's normal role would then revolve more around the universal liaison between churches, the promotion and arbitration of visible communion. He would ever remain the ultimate arbiter of definitions of faith, but would not be burdened to the extent he is today with the practical details of "quasi-imperial government" for the whole Church. *The bishops' conferences* would be responsible for matters of local harmony. Only in exceptional emergency situations would the pope have to intervene as successor of Peter.[242]

Was this not also condemned by Pius VI?

that Jesus Christ willed his Church to be administered after the fashion of a Republic; that it is true the government of the

---

[242] De Roo, "Collegiality and the Petrine Office;"

And Schillebeeckx said: "…there should be a Third Vatican Council to approve papal collegiality (i.e., that the pope is required in conscience – at his discretion, of course – to take into account the world episcopate as accurately as possible). Even so, bishops and theologians were talking about collegiality in a sense that is nowhere reflected in the schema. But the minority – who were not stupid either! – understood well that this diplomatic vagueness in the schema was to be interpreted after the council in the widest possible sense, although the doctrinal commission had not expressly intended nor formulated this in the text itself. The minority was not against collegiality as literally formulated in the text, but against the optimistic perspective that the majority of the doctrinal commission wanted to let resonate therein, deliberately vague and somewhat too diplomatically, without articulating it in the text. Even Congar had long ago objected to a conciliar text deliberately kept vague so that it can be interpreted equivocally. A theologian from the doctrinal commission – to whom I had already complained about the 'minimalism' on papal collegiality during the second session – told me reassuringly, 'We say it diplomatically, but after the Council we will draw the implied conclusions.' I found this to be unfair then, and indeed did not believe in such a conciliar interpretation, whereby one group of voters would take no notice of papal collegiality and the other group would imply it! There should have been either a clear text in which a maximalism (regarding collegiality) was formulated unambiguously, or a clear text in which the older minimalist view (which the schema expressly articulates) was stripped of its equivocal vagueness that concealed the actual problem." Translation and citations Lawrence King, p. 135 of *De Paus: Opvattingen over een omstreden ambt*, ed. Michel van der Plas (Utrecht: Amboboeken, 1965?), pp. 147-56, at 149-50 [originally published in *De Bazuin*, 23 Dec 1964].

Church needs a president for the sake of unity, but that this president must not be permitted to meddle in the affairs of others who govern as he does; that *his whole privilege consists in the right which he has to exhort the negligent to fulfill their duties; that thus, in virtue of his primacy he has no other prerogative than to make up for the negligence of others, and to provide, by his exhortations and his example, for the conservation of unity; that the Popes have no power in another diocese, except in extraordinary cases;* that the Sovereign Pontiff is a Head who has his power and stability from the Church; that the Sovereign Pontiffs have allowed themselves to violate the rights of bishops by reserving to themselves absolutions, dispensations, decisions, appeals, the conferring of benefices…[243]

"Sacrament and Ruling Power Interpenetrate One Another"

Even if Ratzinger would not go as far as De Roo, he was still one of the greatest advocates of collegiality, as he writes:

The rigid juxtaposition of sacrament and *jurisdiction*, of consecrating power and *power of governance*, that had existed since the Middle Ages and was one of the symptoms marking the Western separation of the Churches from the East [the Orthodox], has finally been eliminated… In the eucharistic office, *both the sacrament and the "ruling power" interpenetrate one another*, and it becomes at once clear how inappropriate the words "rule" and "power" are with regard to the Church. We have *no more right to speak of a quasi-profane ruling power, neatly separated from the sacramental ministry, than we have a right to speak of a*

---

[243] *Super Soliditate*

167

separation between the mystical and eucharistic body of Christ."[244]

Again, Ratzinger shows his contempt for the concept of *power associated with office* as in political society. He expresses his wholehearted approval of Vatican II's teaching that not only do bishops receive the power to sanctify when they are ordained, but by that same sacramental consecration, bishops also receive the *power to govern* the flock of Christ—even before they are given "jurisdiction" or "office" (e.g. "Bishop of Paris") by the Pope: "both the sacrament and the 'ruling power' interpenetrate one another..."

Ratzinger explains that one of the chief obstacles between the Catholic Church and the Orthodox churches is now resolved if the powers of the bishop to teach and govern are already given in the sacrament [*potestas ordinis*] of episcopal consecration and not in the *missio canonica* or grant of jurisdiction [*potestas iurisdictionis*] from the Roman Pontiff. The traditional teaching of the Church is that Orthodox bishops have valid sacraments but lack jurisdiction by rejecting the Pope. But *Lumen Gentium* avoided mention of "jurisdiction." Indeed, according to some, it meant to do away with this "ambiguous" word as a *separate* concept altogether.[245]

Bishop Eugenio Corecco agreed with his fellow *Communio* theologian Ratzinger: "In virtue of the [episcopal] consecration which confers a *substrate of jurisdiction* on him in any case, but which, if it is legitimate, also gives him the *communio hierarchica* (which is not identical with the *missio canonica*), *the bishop enters to form a part of the college of bishops.* This is true even if, for any reason, he is not invested with any particular ecclesiastical office

---

[244] Ratzinger, *Theological Highlights,* p. 128.

[245] Guiseppe Alberigo, "The Concept of Jurisdiction in the Catholic Church", ARCIC-134. *Anglican-Roman Catholic Dialogue;* https://iarccum.org/doc/?d=482

and, as a result, does not receive the totality of the power of jurisdiction with the *missio*."[246]

Or, as he says: "...theology has abandoned the thesis that the power of jurisdiction is given to bishops directly by the Pope, in order to take up the more plausible theory according to which jurisdiction is conferred on them by God, whether passing through the mediation of the *missio canonica* conferred by the Pope, or *directly in virtue of episcopal consecration*."[247]

If the power to teach and govern is given at episcopal consecration, and if it is also true that "The order of bishops...is also the subject of supreme and full power over the universal Church," then does the Pope, himself, receive the power to govern the universal Church when he is elected, or when he receives sacramental consecration?[248]

As John Lessard-Thibodeau writes:

Section 21 of the constitution *Lumen gentium* teaches that the power of jurisdiction [power to govern] is received by all bishops in the same way, that is, directly from Christ; *this can only mean the supreme and universal power itself*, the authority of which the College is the subject. Logically, therefore, what can the pope actually receive by his election if not an honorific authority of mere precedence? Therefore, according to this new teaching there is one subject of

---

[246] Bishop Eugenio Corecco, "Nature and Structure of the sacra potestas from the Point of View of Doctrine and in the New Code of Canon Law" (1984); "Natura e struttura della '*Sacra Potestas*' nella dottrina e nel nuovo Codice di diritto canonico," *Communio* (1984), pp. 24-52; https://www.eugeniocorecco.ch

[247] Cf. E. Corecco, "L'origine del potere di giurisdizione...," loc. cit., pp. 10-42, 107-119; https://www.eugeniocorecco.ch

[248] Cf. Gianfranco Ghirlanda, SJ "Cessazione dall'ufficio di Romano Pontefice," *La Civiltà Cattolica*, no. 3905, vol. 1 (March 2, 2013), pp. 445-462; https://www.laciviltacattolica.it/articolo/cessazione-dallufficio-di-romano-pontefice/

supreme authority, namely the College [this is the position of Karl Rahner, Yves Congar, Richard McBrien, and others], of which the pope is only the official spokesman.[249]

Likewise, Bishop Athanasius Schneider has called out the Council's conception of collegiality as an affront to papal prerogatives:

The Synod of Bishops, instituted by Pope Paul VI in 1965 as a permanent structure or an advisory council of bishops on the universal level of the Church, is indeed *a novelty in the entire history of the Church.* The underlying theoretical base for this new structure is the doctrine found in the Vatican II document *Lumen Gentium* (art. 22), according to which there are two permanent supreme subjects or agents in the governing of the universal Church, i.e., the Pope alone and the college of bishops with the Pope. Such a doctrinal affirmation is ambiguous. Although the so-called "Preliminary Note of Explanation" attached to *Lumen Gentium* gave an explanation to avoid an erroneous opinion, there nevertheless remains room for diverging interpretations.[250] *The idea that there are two holders of the*

---

[249] Fr. John G. Lessard-Thibodeau, SSPX; https://fsspx.org/en/coll%C3%A9gialit%C3%A9; Or as Bishop Alfonso Carrasco Rouco writes: "On the other hand, the ministry of the successor of Peter can no longer be understood without a full recognition of the episcopate as the fullness of the sacrament of orders and of its constitutive function for the being of the Church; Consequently, it [the Petrine Ministry] cannot be seen in any way as a superior form of realization of the sacramental order— which would then be inadmissible, *nor as a power of a societal nature that would impose itself above the fullness of the sacramental potestas;*" Alfonso Carrasco Rouco, "La renuncia al Ministerio Petrino," *Scripta theologica: revista de la Facultad de Teología de la Universidad de Navarra*, 45, fasc. 2 (2013), pp. 467-475.

[250] For a summary of these, see Cardinal Luis Tagle, Luis Antonio G. Tagle, "The 'Black Week' of Vatican II (November 14-21, 1964)," in Giuseppe Alberigo, editor. *History of Vatican II.* 5 volumes. Edited by Joseph A. Komonchak; translated by Matthew J. O'Connell. (Maryknoll, NY: Orbis Books, 1995 to 2006), pp. 438-42; John W. O'Malley, *What Happened at Vatican II,* (Cambridge, MA: Harvard University, 2008), pp. 244-245, 367, nt. 140. Citation, Lawrence King.

supreme power in the Church does not correspond to the constant teaching of the Magisterium of the Church. [251]

Nevertheless, Ratzinger, speaking of *Lumen Gentium's* teaching on the Pope and the College of Bishops writes: "To borrow the expression of Heribert Schauf [and Congar], *the Church is not like a circle, with a single center* [the Pope], *but like an ellipse with two foci, primacy and episcopate.*" [252]

As for Pope Paul's "Preliminary Note of Explanation," Ratzinger explains:

> this note injected something of bitterness into the closing days of the session, otherwise so full of valiant hopes [sic]. A detailed analysis of this very intricate text would take us here too far afield. The end result, which is what we are concerned with, would be the realization it did not create any substantially new situation. *Essentially it involved the same **dialectic** and the same **ambiguity** about the real powers of the college as the Council itself manifested.* Without doubt the scales were here further tipped in favor of papal primacy as opposed to collegiality. But for every statement advanced in one direction the text offers one supporting the other side, and this restores the balance, leaving interpretations open in both directions. We can see the text as either "primatialist" or collegial. Thus we can speak of a certain ambivalence in the text of the "explanatory note," reflecting the ambivalent attitude of those who worked on the text and tried to reconcile the conflicting tendencies. The

[251] Bishop Schneider, Matt Gaspers, "Exclusive Bishop Schneider on Synodality" *Catholic Family News* (April 25, 2022); https://catholicfamilynews.com/blog/2022/04/25/exclusive-bishop-schneider-on-synodality/
[252] Karl Rahner and Joseph Ratzinger, *The Episcopate and the Primacy*, Translation Kenneth Barker et al. (New York, NY: Herder and Herder, 1962), p. 43.

consequent ambiguity is a sign that complete harmony of views was neither achieved *nor even possible*. [sic!][253]

Bishop Schneider, who has called for a definitive removal of ambiguity with regard to collegiality (and all other conciliar teaching), has further declared: "Our Lord Jesus Christ instituted Peter as the only supreme personal shepherd of His entire flock, including both *clergy* and faithful. Peter is also the only rock upon which Christ built His Church (cf. Matt. 16:18). There are not two rocks or two supreme shepherds, i.e., a personal rock and on his side a collegial rock, or a personal supreme subject (shepherd) and on his side a collegial supreme subject (shepherd)."[254]

It should be noted that Bishop Schneider (and Archbishop Vigano—and the lay faithful) are within their rights to question the Council's teaching on collegiality (and other novelties). In a stunning admission, Ratzinger, himself, confesses that the teaching of *Lumen Gentium* on collegiality is NOT a dogma. Before the final vote on *LG* was taken, Cardinal Pericle Felici, the General Secretary of the Council, offered a *"Qualificatio theologica"* regarding its theological weight (and the weight, for that matter, of all the documents of Vatican II): "Taking into account conciliar custom and the pastoral aim of the present council, *this holy synod defines as binding on the church only those matters concerning faith and morals which it openly declares to be such."* Citing this, Ratzinger writes:

"This is not the case anywhere in the text we have analyzed (nos. 19-22 of Chapter 3 of the Constitution [*LG*]). *Therefore they contain no new dogma.*" He says that the assertion of the sacramentality of the episcopal office "most nearly

[253] Ratzinger, *Theological Highlights*, p. 115.

[254] Matt Gaspers, Bishop Schneider, "Exclusive Bishop Schneider on Synodality." *Catholic Family News* (April 25, 2022); https://catholicfamilynews.com/blog/2022/04/25/exclusive-bishop-schneider-on-synodality/

approaches being a dogma," because of the solemnity of the introductory words "This sacred Council teaches," but even it should not be considered a dogma, for the text does not state that this doctrine is part of the apostolic deposit of faith, *nor that it be received with the assent of faith.*[255] Nevertheless, Ratzinger, has never wavered in his promulgation of the Council's teaching that the bishop's power to govern (and teach and sanctify) originates in his sacramental consecration, in which case, "jurisdiction" is never truly separate, it always has a sacramental basis—not given by the Pope.

As he says: *"The ministry of the bishop is not an externally assigned 'administrative power,'* but rather arises from the necessary plurality of the eucharistic communities (i.e., of the Churches in the Church) and, as representing these, *is itself sacramentally based. The ruling of the Church and its spiritual mystery are inseparable."*[256]

Or as Corecco puts it: **"If it is true that the *potestas sacra* can be transmitted only through the sacrament of Orders,** it **follows that it** *cannot be transmitted in another way even when it*

---

[255] Joseph Ratzinger, "La collégialité épiscopale, développement théologique," Translation into French by R. Virrion, in *L'Église de Vatican II: Études autour de la Constitution conciliare sur l'Église,* vol. 2, ed. Guilherme Baraúna, French edition ed. Yves M-J. Congar (Paris: Cerf, 1966), pp. 763-90; 789. Original text: "Ce n'est le cas nulle part dans la partie du texte que nous avons analysée, les no. 19-22 du chapitre III de la Constitution. Ils ne contiennent aucun dogme nouveau, par conséquent. On a le sentiment que le passage (III, no 21, a. 2) qui énonce la sacramentalité de la charge épiscopale est celui qui approche le plus de la qualification dogmatique....". "The final words of this paragraph refer to the assent of faith in the original German [zur glaubensmäßigen Annahme gestellt] and in the Italian [assenso della fede]; the French translation is not completely accurate here." Joseph Ratzinger, "Die bischöfliche Kollegialität: Theologische Entfaltung," in *De Ecclesia: Beitr ge ur onstitution " ber die rche" des weiten Vatikanischen on ils,* vol. 2, ed. Guilherme Baraúna; German edition ed.). Semmelroth, J. G. Gerhartz, and H. Vorgrimler (Freiburg: Herder, 1966), pp. 44-70, at). 69; idem, "La collegialità episcopale: spiegazione teologica del testo conciliare," Translation into Italian by [no first name] Olivieri, in *La Chiesa del Vaticano II: Studi e ommenti intorno alla Constituzione dommatica "Lumen gentium",* ed. Guilherme Baraúna Florence: Vallechi, 1965), pp. 733-60, at p. 759. Commentary, translation and citation, Lawrence King, p. 129.

[256] Ratzinger, *Theological Highlights,* pp. 189-190.

is manifested according to the logic of the power of jurisdiction."[257]

Papacy as Fullness of Sacrament of Orders?

But where does this leave the sacred power exercised by the Bishop of Rome, which for centuries has been considered an office of jurisdiction only? Is it too *sacramentally based*? Because, as Ratzinger argues, the *"ruling of the Church and its spiritual mystery are inseparable"*? This would explain Benedict renouncing ruling as Bishop of Rome, yet paradoxically remaining "Pope" in some real sense.

As Cardinal Gianfranco Ghirlanda, Emeritus Professor of Canon Law and former rector of the Pontifical Gregorian University of Rome[258] observes, this question was taken up (without doctrinal finality) by the Commission for the development of the current Code of Canon Law in 1981:

The other doctrinal line present in the Commission stated that the acceptance of the [papal] election is not sufficient for the elect to obtain full and supreme power, but episcopal consecration is also necessary. The arguments presented were the following:
1) the dogmatic Constitution *Lumen gentium* (*LG* abolished the distinction between power of order and power of jurisdiction, teaching the unity between consecration and jurisdiction, and therefore that ecclesiastical power derives from consecration;
2) in this way a split between the charismatic Church and the juridical Church is avoided;

[257] https://www.eugeniocorecco.ch/scritti/scritti-scientifici/canon-law-and-communio/canon-law-and-communio-10/#14
[258] Bergoglio favored him with the Cardinal's hat in August 2022, even though he is not a bishop.

3) if consecration is required to be a member of the episcopal college, this requirement *a fortiori* applies to the head of the college.[259]

Ghirlanda, himself, does not agree with this ecclesiology, however, because

The greatest difficulty that arises from the affirmation that the primatial power of the Roman Pontiff comes from the episcopal consecration and not from the acceptance of the election would be that, on the one hand, it would not be seen how to explain what is affirmed by *LG* 22a, by *NEP* 1 and by Paul VI and, on the other hand, that, *in the event that the Pope resigns from his office not because of death, he would never lose this power, as it is conferred by a sacramental act which has an indelible character.*[260]

According to the logic of the *communio* school of thought, when the Pope receives "power" or "jurisdiction" over the universal Church, this Petrine ministry being "sacramentally based" is seemingly irrevocable. As Ratzinger said in his Last General Audience: "Always—anyone who accepts the Petrine ministry no longer has any privacy. He belongs always and completely to everyone, to the whole Church...The 'always' is also a 'forever'—there is no longer a return to the private. *My decision to renounce the active exercise of the ministry does not revoke this.*"[261]

---

[259] G. Ghirlanda, "Cessazione dall'ufficio di Romano Pontefice;" Cf. Pontificio Consiglio per i Testi Legislativi, *Congregatio Plenaria diebus 20-29 octobris 1981 habita*, (Città del Vaticano, 1991), pp. 365-366.

[260] G. Ghirlanda, SJ "Cessazione dall'ufficio di Romano Pontefice"; https://www.laciviltacattolica.it/articolo/cessazione-dallufficio-di-romano-pontefice/

[261] https://www.vatican.va/content/benedict-xvi/en/audiences/2013/documents/hf_ben-xvi_aud_20130227.html

Are Order and Jurisdiction Distinct?

Because of this radical result, let us delve more deeply into the competition between the semi-traditional and progressive ecclesiologies in the postconciliar Church:

> ...on the question of the *sacra potestas* in the Church there are two great interpretations based on the origin of the power of the bishops. On the one hand, the conception of sacramental power as originating from the sacrament of Holy Orders (cf. W. Bertrams, G. Philips, K. Morsdorf, W. Aymans, K. Rahner, Y. Congar, E. Corecco, J. Manzanares...) and on the other, as participated through the sacrament [episcopal consecration] *and* the ecclesial mission [*missio canonica* granted by the Pope] (cf. D. Staffa, A. Gutiérrez, U. Lattanzi, A.M. Stickler, J. Beyer, G. Ghirlanda...). *Starting from an ecclesiology of communion* and a better knowledge of the Decree of Gratian (1120-1140), it is possible to try to overcome the *ordo/iurisdictio* dualism by the *potestas/executio* unit, in which *all power is transmitted by the sacrament of orders*"[262]

Péter Szabo agrees:

> As it is well-known, the origin of episcopal power is interpreted by contemporary Catholic doctrine in (partially) different terms from the model that has evolved since the 12th century. According to the earlier conception, "jurisdiction" was considered to be of extra-sacramental origin, in other words, transmissible independently of episcopal ordination. A subtle distinction between the sanctifying and jurisdictional dimensions of power is

---

[262] Christopher O'Donnell, Salvador Pié-Ninot, *Diccionario de Eclesiología*, (Madrid, 2001), pp. 484–501.

appropriate (since it is required by the practicalities of life), and some of its traces are even detectable in former tradition.[263] However, medieval doctrine, as we know, not only differentiated but professed full separation of the two realities as well. According to this theory only power of order derives from episcopal ordination, *whereas the source of all forms of jurisdiction is exclusively the papal office. In consequence of this (sacramentally inaccurate) starting point, jurisdictional power assumed a one-sidedly "vertical" character in the medieval ecclesiological model.* This deviation would be corrected only in the second half of the last century thanks to the recognition that *ecclesiastical power (as sacred reality) is in its entirety of sacramental origin.* As Mörsdorf emphasised after the Council *"order and jurisdiction cannot be considered two separate powers but complementary elements of the one ecclesiastical power".*[264] Thus,

---

[263] Cf. Pierre L'Huillier, "Rapport entre pouvoirs d'ordre et de juridiction dans la tradition orientale", in *Revue de Droit Canonique* 23 (1973), pp. 281–289; Cf. also: Orazio Condorelli, La distinzione tra potestà di ordine e potestà di giurisdizione nella tradizione canonica bizantina, in *Episcopal Ordination and Episcopal Ministry according to Catholic and Orthodox Doctrine and Canon Law*, Faculty of Theology of the University of Fribourg, Switzerland, April 3–6, 2013; Roberto Interlandi, *Potestà sacramentale e potestà di governo nel primo millennio: esercizio di esse e loro distinzione*, (Tesi Gregoriana DC 103), (Roma 2016); Citations from Szabó, p. 3.

[264] Cf. Decree on the Bishops' Pastoral Office in the Church [commented by Klaus Mörsdorf], in *Commentary on the Documents of Vatican II*, Herbert Vorgrimler (ed.), (New York 1966–69), vol. II, p. 207. For an overview of the different interpretations on the relationship between LG 23 and NEP, see for example: Adriano Celeghin, *Origine e natura della potestà sacra: posizioni postconciliari*, Brescia 1987; Gianfranco Ghirlanda, "Potestà sacra", in *Nuovo dizionario di diritto canonico*, Carlos C. Salvador – Velasio De Paolis – Gianfranco Ghirlanda (a cura di),(Milano, 1993), pp. 803–812; Francesco Viscome, *Origine ed esercizio della potestà dei vescovi dal Vaticano I al Vaticano II. Contesto teologico-canonico del magistero dei «recenti pontefici». Nota explicatriva praevia* 2 (Tesi Gregoriana DC 21), (Roma, 1997). Although it is true that the Explanatory Note (NEP) clarifies this statement, in any case, it does not modify it in merit, since the "effective cause" of the sacred power according to the intention of the conciliar text *remains the only ordination,*

governing power ('jurisdiction') also derives from episcopal ordination or, at least, has its roots in it.[265]

Or as Msgr. Fredrik Hansen describes it:

The first current emanates from...K. Rahner, *J. Ratzinger* and Y. Congar...They all support the view that *potestas sacra* comes from the sacrament of orders. *In the case of the potestas sacra of the Bishop they advocate its complete origin in episcopal consecration...Further this position teaches that also the power of teaching and governance comes from episcopal ordination* although its exercise must take place within hierarchical communion. The [papal] *missio canonica* as the juridical determination for the two latter powers [teaching and governing] renders this *potestas sacra* available for its exercise...*The Primacy of jurisdiction of the Supreme Pontiff (cf. can. 331, PAE chap III, LG 18b) becomes difficult to explain in relation to this current. On a sacramental level (the power of order) there is no difference between the Roman Pontiff and the other Bishops of the Church.* The difference in jurisdiction comes from a non-sacramental source...The power he then acquires comes directly from Christ, not from the election, and not from the College of Cardinals.[266]

---

264 (footnote cont'd) while the hierarchical communion or missio canonica is only an additive *conditio sine qua non*; see: Gérard Philips, *La Chiesa e il suo mistero. Storia, testo e commento della Lumen gentium,* (Milano 1989, 226; Umberto Betti, *La dottrina sull'Episcopato nel capitolo III della costituzione dommatica Lumen gentium. Sussidio per la lettura del testo,* (Roma, 1968), p, 365; Citations from Péter Szabó, *"Synodality" – Dimensions of an Ecclesiological and Canonical Concept in Ecumenical Perspective Towards a Common Sacramental Understanding? https://www.unifr.ch/orthodoxia/de/assets/public/files/Dokumentation/Synodality/Introduction_Szabó.pdf*

265 Szabó, p 3.

266 Frederik Hansen, *The Unity and Threefold Expression of the Potestas Regiminis of the Diocesan Bishop,* (Rome: Gregorian & Biblical Press, 2014), pp. 25-26.

Hansen contrasts this view with "The second current of thought...[which] makes a distinction between the episcopal consecration [*ordinis*] on the one hand and the *missio canonica* [*iurisdictionis*] on the other. The result is a position diametrically opposed to the first [Ratzinger's] school of thought, holding that the power of governance comes from the *missio canonica* by which *an office is entrusted...it allows an explanation of the difference between the Pope and the Bishops as regards jurisdiction.*[267]

To which Bishop Carrasco Rouco would respond:

Indeed, this ecclesiology is characterized by a particular conception of the *sacra potestas*, that of a distinction between the sacramental power (of order) and that of jurisdiction. Now, **such a duality implies a separation between the legal and sacramental dimensions of ecclesial reality,** an operation at the end of which, however, priority *will once again return to jurisdiction; one thus develops a conception of law in the Church, and,* **in particular, of the papal primacy,** *which loses sight of the* **sacramentality of the episcopate, and which also tends to reduce the space of collegiality.** We thus build on bases other than those of the *ecclesiology of communion.*[268]

In a footnote [Nt. 284] he cites Ratzinger's agreement with him on the subject: "The consequences of this dual power...[Cf.] J. Ratzinger, 'Die bischofliche Kollegialitat' in *De Ecclesia*, Von G. Barauna."

As we see with the above quotes, Ratzinger is a theologian who insists on the priority of the sacramental over the juridical. In

---

[267] Hansen, p. 25.

[268] Alfonso Carrasco Rouco, *Le Primat de L'Eveque de Rome, Studia Friburgensia Nouvelle Serie* 73, Sectio Canonica 7, (Editions Universitaires Fribourg Suisse, 1990), p. 03. My translation from the Spanish.

his *Principles of Catholic Theology*, he even appears to apply this to the papacy. Expressing his sympathy for the view of the Orthodox churches, Ratzinger writes:

Precisely this difference in the concept...grew...[up to] 1870 with the proclamation of the primacy of jurisdiction: in one case [traditional Orthodox view], only the tradition that has been handed down serves as a valid source of law, and only the consensus of all is the normative criterion for determining and interpreting it. In the other case [traditional Catholic view], the source of law appears to be the will of the sovereign, which creates on its own authority (*ex sese*) new laws that then have the power to bind. The old sacramental structure seems overgrown, *even choked, by this new concept of law: the papacy is not a sacrament, it is "only" a juridical institution; but this juridical institution has set itself above the sacramental order.*[269]

That Ratzinger believes that papal power is sacramental explains both what he renounced and what is irrevocable in "Pope Emeritus."

---

[269] Ratzinger, *Principles of Catholic Theology*, pp. 194-195; As Szabó writes: "The above thesis of simultaneity makes it possible and even demands that, *in the Catholic ecclesiological paradigm, the heuristic cornerstone be no longer exclusively the jurisdictional primacy. The Petrine function should be interpreted in the framework of the doctrine of communion instead.* In this context...the goal of ecumenical dialogue would no longer be the full recognition of the universal jurisdiction of the pope by the Orthodox in terms of purely juridical categories;" "Synodality and Primacy Perspectives of Interaction between East and West;" "Synodality and Primacy Perspectives of Interaction between East and West" in *Primacy and Synodality: Deepening Insights Proceedings of the 23rd Congress of the Society for the Law of the Eastern Churches Debrecen*, September 3–8, 2017, edited by Péter Szabó (*Kanon* XXV, Nyíregyháza 2019), pp. 693–722; 702. Ratzinger: "The essence of the primacy as outlined by the First and Second Vatican Councils: The pope is not an absolute monarch *whose will is law*; rather, he is the guardian of the authentic Tradition and, thereby, the premier guarantor of obedience," "Preface," in Dom Alcuin Reid, *The Organic Development of the Liturgy*, (San Francisco, CA: Ignatius Press, 2005), p. 10.

Appendix II
Purported Text of the Third Secret of Fatima

«J.M.J.

The third part of the secret revealed at the Cova da Iria-Fatima, on 13 July 1917.

I write in obedience to you, my God, who command me to do so through his Excellency the Bishop of Leiria and through your Most Holy Mother and mine.

After the two parts which I have already explained, at the left of Our Lady and a little above, we saw an Angel with a flaming sword in his left hand; flashing, it gave out flames that looked as though they would set the world on fire; but they died out in contact with the splendour that Our Lady radiated towards him from her right hand: pointing to the earth with his right hand, the Angel cried out in a loud voice: 'Penance, Penance, Penance!'. And we saw in an immense light that is God: 'something similar to how people appear in a mirror when they pass in front of it' a Bishop dressed in White 'we had the impression that it was the Holy Father'. Other Bishops, Priests, men and women Religious going up a steep mountain, at the top of which there was a big Cross of rough-hewn trunks as of a cork-tree with the bark; before reaching there the Holy Father passed through a big city half in ruins and half trembling with halting step, afflicted with pain and sorrow, he prayed for the souls of the corpses he met on his way; having reached the top of the mountain, on his knees at the foot of the big Cross he was killed by a group of soldiers who fired bullets and arrows at him, and in the same way there died one after another the other Bishops, Priests, men and women Religious, and various lay people of different ranks and positions. Beneath the two arms of the Cross there were two Angels each with a crystal aspersorium in his hand, in which they gathered up the blood of the Martyrs and with it sprinkled the souls that were making their way to God.

Tuy-3-1-1944».

Appendix III
Pope Benedict's *Declaratio*
English Translation

Dear Brothers,

I have convoked you to this Consistory, not only for the three canonizations, but also to communicate to you a decision of great importance for the life of the Church. After having repeatedly examined my conscience before God, I have come to the certainty that my strengths, due to an advanced age, are no longer suited to an adequate exercise of the Petrine ministry. I am well aware that this ministry, due to its essential spiritual nature, must be carried out not only with words and deeds, but no less with prayer and suffering. However, in today's world, subject to so many rapid changes and shaken by questions of deep relevance for the life of faith, in order to govern the barque of Saint Peter and proclaim the Gospel, both strength of mind and body are necessary, strength which in the last few months, has deteriorated in me to the extent that I have had to recognize my incapacity to adequately fulfill the ministry entrusted to me. For this reason, and well aware of the seriousness of this act, with full freedom I declare that I renounce the ministry of Bishop of Rome, Successor of Saint Peter, entrusted to me by the Cardinals on 19 April 2005, in such a way, that as from 28 February 2013, at 20:00 hours, the See of Rome, the See of Saint Peter, will be vacant and a Conclave to elect the new Supreme Pontiff will have to be convoked by those whose competence it is.

Dear Brothers, I thank you most sincerely for all the love and work with which you have supported me in my ministry and I ask pardon for all my defects. And now, let us entrust the Holy Church to the care of Our Supreme Pastor, Our Lord Jesus Christ, and implore his holy Mother Mary, so that she may assist the

Cardinal Fathers with her maternal solicitude, in electing a new Supreme Pontiff. With regard to myself, I wish to also devotedly serve the Holy Church of God in the future through a life dedicated to prayer.

From the Vatican, 10 February 2013

BENEDICTUS PP XVI

Pope Benedict's *Declaratio*
Latin Original

Fratres carissimi

Non solum propter tres canonizationes ad hoc Consistorium vos convocavi, sed etiam ut vobis decisionem magni momenti pro Ecclesiae vita communicem. Conscientia mea iterum atque iterum coram Deo explorata ad cognitionem certam perveni vires meas ingravescente aetate non iam aptas esse ad munus Petrinum aeque administrandum.

Bene conscius sum hoc munus secundum suam essentiam spiritualem non solum agendo et loquendo exsequi debere, sed non minus patiendo et orando. Attamen in mundo nostri temporis rapidis mutationibus subiecto et quaestionibus magni ponderis pro vita fidei perturbato ad navem Sancti Petri gubernandam et ad annuntiandum Evangelium etiam vigor quidam corporis et animae necessarius est, qui ultimis mensibus in me modo tali minuitur, ut incapacitatem meam ad ministerium mihi commissum bene administrandum agnoscere debeam. Quapropter bene conscius ponderis huius actus plena libertate declaro me ministerio Episcopi Romae, Successoris Sancti Petri, mihi per manus Cardinalium die 19 aprilis MMV commisso renuntiare ita ut a die 28 februarii MMXIII, hora 20, sedes Romae, sedes Sancti Petri vacet et Conclave ad eligendum novum Summum Pontificem ab his quibus competit convocandum esse.

Fratres carissimi, ex toto corde gratias ago vobis pro omni amore et labore, quo mecum pondus ministerii mei portastis et veniam peto pro omnibus defectibus meis. Nunc autem Sanctam Dei Ecclesiam curae Summi eius Pastoris, Domini nostri Iesu Christi confidimus sanctamque eius Matrem Mariam imploramus, ut patribus Cardinalibus in eligendo novo Summo Pontifice materna sua bonitate assistat. Quod ad me attinet etiam in futuro vita orationi dedicata Sanctae Ecclesiae Dei toto ex corde servire velim.

Ex Aedibus Vaticanis, die 10 mensis februarii MMXIII

BENEDICTUS PP. XVI

Appendix IV
Pope Benedict's Last General Audience Address

Venerable Brothers in the Episcopate and in the Presbyterate!
Distinguished Authorities!
Dear Brothers and Sisters!

I thank all of you for having come in such great numbers to this last General Audience.

Heartfelt thanks! I am truly moved and I see the Church alive! And I think we should also says thanks to the Creator for the fine weather which he gives us even on this winter day.

Like the Apostle Paul in the biblical text which we have heard, I too feel a deep need first and foremost to thank God, who gives guidance and growth to the Church, who sows his word and thus nourishes faith in his people. At this moment my heart expands and embraces the whole Church throughout the world; and I thank God for all that I have "heard" in these years of the Petrine ministry about the faith in the Lord Jesus Christ and the love which truly circulates in the Body of the Church and makes it live in love, and about the hope which opens and directs us towards the fullness of life, towards our heavenly homeland.

I feel that I bear everyone in prayer, in a present, God's present, in which I gather together every one of my meetings, journeys and pastoral visits. In prayer I gather each and all, in order to entrust them to the Lord: that we might be filled with the knowledge of his will, with all spiritual wisdom and understanding, and that we might lead a life worthy of him and of his love, bearing fruit in every good work (cf. *Col* 1:9-10).

At this moment I feel great confidence, because I know, we all know, that the Gospel word of truth is the Church's strength, it is her life. The Gospel purifies and renews, it bears fruit, wherever the community of believers hears it and receives God's grace in truth and charity. This is my confidence, this is my joy.

When on 19 April nearly eight years ago I accepted the Petrine ministry, I had the firm certainty that has always accompanied me: this certainty of the life of the Church which comes from the word of God. At that moment, as I have often said, the words which echoed in my heart were: Lord, why are you asking this of me, and what is it that you are asking of me? It is a heavy burden which you are laying on my shoulders, but if you ask it of me, at your word I will cast the net, sure that you will lead me even with all my weaknesses. And eight years later I can say that the Lord has truly led me, he has been close to me, I have been able to perceive his presence daily. It has been a portion of the Church's journey which has had its moments of joy and light, but also moments which were not easy; I have felt like Saint Peter with the Apostles in the boat on the Sea of Galilee: the Lord has given us so many days of sun and of light winds, days when the catch was abundant; there were also moments when the waters were rough and the winds against us, as throughout the Church's history, and the Lord seemed to be sleeping. But I have always known that the Lord is in that boat, and I have always known that the barque of the Church is not mine but his. Nor does the Lord let it sink; it is he who guides it, surely also through those whom he has chosen, because he so wished. This has been, and is, a certainty which nothing can shake. For this reason my heart todays overflows with gratitude to God, for he has never let his Church, or me personally, lack his consolation, his light, his love.

We are in the *Year of Faith* which I desired precisely to reaffirm our faith in God in a context which seems to push him more and more into the background. I should like to invite all of us to renew our firm confidence in the Lord, to entrust ourselves like children in God's arms, certain that those arms always hold us, enabling us to press forward each day, even when the going is rough. I want everyone to feel loved by that God who gave his Son for us and who has shown us his infinite love. I want everyone to feel the joy of being a Christian. In one beautiful morning prayer, it says: "I adore you, my God, and I love you with all my heart. I thank you for having created me and made me a Christian...". Yes, we are happy for the gift of faith; it is our most precious possession, which no one can take from us! Let us thank the Lord for this daily, in prayer and by a consistent Christian life. God loves us, but he also expects us to love him!

But it is not only God whom I want to thank at this moment. The Pope is not alone in guiding the barque of Peter, even if it is his first responsibility. I have never felt alone in bearing the joy and the burden of the Petrine ministry; the Lord has set beside me so many people who, with generosity and love for God and the Church, have helped me and been close to me. Above all you, dear brother Cardinals: your wisdom, your counsel and your friendship have been invaluable to me; my co-workers, beginning with my Secretary of State who has faithfully accompanied me in these years; the Secretariat of State and the whole Roman Curia, as well as all those who in various sectors offer their service to the Holy See: many, many unseen faces which remain in the background, but precisely through their silent, daily dedication in a spirit of faith and humility they have been a sure and trustworthy support to me. I also think in a special way of the Church of Rome, my Diocese! I cannot forget my Brothers in the Episcopate and in the Presbyterate, the consecrated persons and the entire People of God: in my pastoral visits, meetings, audiences and journeys I have always felt great kindness and deep affection; yet I too have felt affection for each and all without distinction, with that pastoral charity which is the heart of every Pastor, and especially of the Bishop of Rome, the Successor of the Apostle Peter. Every day I have borne each of you in prayer, with the heart of a father.

I would like my greeting and my thanksgiving to extend to everyone: the heart of the Pope reaches out to the whole world. And I wish to express my gratitude to the Diplomatic Corps accredited to the Holy See which represents the great family of the nations. Here I think too of all those who work for good communications and I thank them for their important service.

At this point, I would also like to thank most heartily all those people throughout the world who in these recent weeks have sent me moving expressions of concern, friendship and prayer. Yes, the Pope is never alone; now I once again experience this so overwhelmingly that my heart is touched. The Pope belongs to everyone and so many persons feel very close to him. It is true that I receive letters from world leaders – from heads of state, from religious leaders, from representatives of the world of culture, and so on. But I also receive many many letters from ordinary people who write to me simply and from the heart, and who show me their affection, an affection born of our being together with Christ Jesus, in the Church. These people do not write to me in the way one writes, for example, to a prince or some important person whom they do not know. They write to me as brothers and sisters, as sons and daughters, with a sense of a very affectionate family bond. Here one can sense palpably what the Church is – not an organization, an association for religious or humanitarian ends, but a living body, a communion of brothers and sisters in the Body of Christ, which makes us all one. To experience the Church in this way and to be able as it were to put one's finger on the strength of her truth and her love, is a cause for joy at a time when so many people are speaking of her decline. But we see how the Church is alive today!

In these last months I have felt my energies declining, and I have asked God insistently in prayer to grant me his light and to help me make the right decision, not for my own good, but for the good of the Church. I have taken this step with full awareness of its gravity and even its novelty, but with profound interior serenity. Loving the Church means also having the courage to make difficult, painful decisions, always looking to the good of the Church and not of oneself.

Here, allow me to go back once again to 19 April 2005. The real gravity of the decision was also due to the fact that from that moment on I was engaged always and forever by the Lord. Always – anyone who accepts the Petrine ministry no longer has any privacy. He belongs always and completely to everyone, to the whole Church. In a manner of speaking, the private dimension of his life is completely eliminated. I was able to experience, and I experience it even now, that one receives one's life precisely when one gives it away. Earlier I said that many people who love the Lord also love the Successor of Saint Peter and feel great affection for him; that the Pope truly has brothers and sisters, sons and daughters, throughout the world, and that he feels secure in the embrace of your communion; because he no longer belongs to himself, he belongs to all and all belong to him.

The "always" is also a "for ever" – there can no longer be a return to the private sphere. My decision to resign the active exercise of the ministry does not revoke this. I do not return to private life, to a life of travel, meetings, receptions, conferences, and so on. I am not abandoning the cross, but remaining in a new way at the side of the crucified Lord. I no longer bear the power of office for the governance of the Church, but in the service of prayer I remain, so to speak, in the enclosure of Saint Peter. Saint Benedict, whose name I bear as Pope, will be a great example for me in this. He showed us the way for a life which, whether active or passive, is completely given over to the work of God.

I also thank each and every one of you for the respect and understanding with which you have accepted this important decision. I will continue to accompany the Church's journey with prayer and reflection, with that devotion to the Lord and his Bride which I have hitherto sought to practise daily and which I would like to practise always. I ask you to remember me in prayer before God, and above all to pray for the Cardinals, who are called to so weighty a task, and for the new Successor of the Apostle Peter. may the Lord accompany him with the light and strength of his Spirit.

Let us call upon the maternal intercession of the Virgin Mary, Mother of God and Mother of the Church, that she may accompany each of us and the whole ecclesial community; to her let us commend ourselves with deep confidence.

Dear friends! God guides his Church, he sustains it always, especially at times of difficulty. Let us never lose this vision of faith, which is the one true way of looking at the journey of the Church and of the world. In our hearts, in the heart of each of you, may there always abide the joyful certainty that the Lord is at our side: he does not abandon us, he remains close to us and he surrounds us with his love. Thank you!

Appendix V
Archbishop Georg Gänswein's "Expanded Petrine Ministry" Address
Pontifical Gregorian University May 20, 2016

(My translation from the Italian original, https://
www.acistampa.com/story/bendetto-xvi-la-fine-del-vecchio-
linizio-del-nuovo-lanalisi-di-georg-ganswein-3369)

Eminences, Excellencies, dear Brothers, Ladies and Gentlemen!

In one of the last conversations the Pope's biographer, Peter Seewald of Munich, was able to have with Benedict XVI, in taking his leave he asked him, "Are you the end of the old or the beginning of the new?" The Pope's answer was short and sure: "One and the other," he replied.

The tape recorder was already turned off; that is why this last exchange of lines is not found in any of Peter Seewald's interview books, not even in the famous *Light of the World*. They are found only in an interview, which he gave to *Corriere della Sera* in the aftermath of Benedict XVI's *Declaration of Renunciation*, in which the biographer remembered those key words that figure somewhat as a maxim in Roberto Regoli's book.

Indeed, I must admit that it is perhaps impossible to sum up more concisely the pontificate of Benedict XVI. And this is affirmed by those who over all these years have had the privilege of closely experiencing this Pope as a classic "*homo historicus,*" the Western man par excellence who has embodied the richness of the Catholic tradition like no other; and who - at the same time - has been so bold as to open the door to a new phase, for that historical turning point that no one five years ago could have imagined. Since then we have been living in a historical epoch that is unprecedented in the bimillennial history of the Church.

As in Peter's time, today the one, holy, catholic and apostolic Church continues to have only one legitimate pope. And yet, for the past three years, we live with two living successors of Peter among us -- who are not in a competitive relationship with each other, and yet both with an extraordinary presence! We might add that the spirit of Joseph Ratzinger earlier already decisively marked the long pontificate of St. John Paul II, whom he faithfully served for almost a quarter of a century as Prefect of the Congregation for the Doctrine of the Faith. Many continue to perceive even today this new situation as a kind of "state of exception" willed by Heaven.

But is it already time to take stock of Benedict XVI's pontificate? In general, in Church history, only ex post popes can be judged and framed correctly. And as proof of this, Regoli himself mentions the case of Gregory VII, the great reforming pope of the Middle Ages, who at the end of his life died in exile in Salerno - as a failure, in the judgment of so many of his contemporaries. And yet, it was precisely Gregory VII who, amid the controversies of his time, decisively shaped the face of the Church for the generations that followed. All the more daring, therefore, seems to be Professor Regoli today in attempting to draw already a balance of the pontificate of Benedict XVI while still living.

The amount of critical material he has viewed and analyzed for this purpose is mighty and impressive. In fact, Benedict XVI is and remains extraordinarily present with his writings as well: both those produced as pope - the three books on Jesus of Nazareth and sixteen (!) volumes of Teachings he delivered to us during his pontificate - and as Professor Ratzinger or Cardinal Ratzinger, whose works could fill a small library.

And so, this work by Regoli has no shortage of footnotes, as numerous as the memories it awakens in me. For I was present when Benedict XVI, at the end of his term, laid down his Fisherman's ring, as is customary in the aftermath of a pope's death, although in this case he was still living! I was present when he, on the other hand, decided not to renounce the name he had chosen, as Pope Celestine V had done when he had become Peter of Morrone again on December 13, 1294, a few months after the beginning of his ministry.

Therefore, as of February 11, 2013, the papal ministry is no longer what it was before. It is and remains the foundation of the Catholic Church; and yet it is a foundation that Benedict XVI has profoundly and enduringly transformed in his pontificate of exception (*Ausnahmepontifikat*), in comparison to which the sober Cardinal Sodano, reacting with immediacy and simplicity immediately after the surprising *Declaration of Renunciation*, deeply moved and almost taken aback, had exclaimed that that news had resounded among the assembled cardinals "like a bolt from the blue." It was on the morning of that same day when, in the evening, a kilometer-long bolt of lightning with an incredible roar struck the tip of the dome of St. Peter's placed above the tomb of the Prince of the Apostles. Rarely has the cosmos accompanied an historical turning point more dramatically. But on the morning of that Feb. 11, Dean of the College of Cardinals Angelo Sodano concluded his rebuttal to Benedict XVI's *Declaration* with an early and similarly cosmic assessment of the pontificate when he finally said, "Certainly, the stars in the sky will always continue to shine and so will always shine in our midst the star of his pontificate."

Equally brilliant and enlightening is Fr. Regoli's thorough and well-documented exposition of the different phases of the pontificate. Especially of the beginning of it in the conclave of

April 2005, from which Joseph Ratzinger, after one of the shortest elections in Church history, came out elected after only four ballots following a dramatic struggle between the so-called "Salt of Earth Party" around Cardinals López Trujíllo, Ruini, Herranz, Rouco Varela or Medina and the so-called "St. Gallen Group" around Cardinals Danneels, Martini, Silvestrini or Murphy-O'Connor; a group that, recently, Cardinal Danneels of Brussels himself amusedly described as "a kind of mafia-club." The election was certainly the outcome also of a clash, the key to which Ratzinger himself had almost provided as cardinal dean, in his historic homily on April 18, 2005, in St. Peter's; and precisely there where to "a dictatorship of relativism that recognizes nothing as definitive and that leaves as the ultimate measure only one's own self and its cravings" he had contrasted another measure: "the Son of God and true man" as "the measure of true humanism." This part of Regoli's intelligent analysis today reads almost like a breathtaking detective story from not too long ago; while instead the "dictatorship of relativism" has long been overwhelmingly expressed through the many channels of new media that, in 2005, could hardly be imagined.

Already the name the new pope gave himself immediately after his election therefore represented a program. Joseph Ratzinger did not become John Paul III, as perhaps many would have hoped. Instead, he harkened back to Benedict XV - the unheard of and unfortunate great peace pope of the terrible years of World War I - and to St. Benedict of Norcia, patriarch of monasticism and patron saint of Europe. I could appear as a superwitness to testify how, in earlier years, never had Cardinal Ratzinger pressed to rise to the highest office in the Catholic Church.

Instead, he already dreamed vividly of a condition that would allow him to write in peace and quiet some, last books. Everyone knows that things turned out differently. During the election, then, in the Sistine Chapel I was a witness that he experienced the election as a "real shock" and felt "turmoil," and that he felt "like getting dizzy" as soon as he realized that "the axe" of election would fall on him. I am not revealing any secrets here because it was Benedict XVI himself who confessed all this publicly at the first audience granted to the pilgrims who had come from Germany. And so it is not surprising that it was Benedict XVI who was the first pope who immediately after his election invited the faithful to pray for him, a fact that again this book reminds us of.

Regoli sketches the different years of ministry in a fascinating and moving way, evoking the mastery and confidence with which Benedict XVI exercised his mandate. And that emerged from the very moment, a few months after his election, when he invited for a private conversation both his longtime, fierce antagonist Hans Küng and Oriana Fallaci, the agnostic and combative grand dame of Jewish origin of the Italian secular media; or when he appointed Werner Arber, Swiss evangelical and Nobel laureate, the first non-Catholic president of the Pontifical Academy of Social Sciences. Regoli does not suppress the accusation of lack of knowledge of men that has often been levelled at the brilliant Theologian in the role of the Fisherman; capable of genially evaluating difficult texts and books and who nevertheless, in 2010, frankly confided to Peter Seewald how difficult he found decisions about people because "no one can read into the heart of the other." How true!

Rightly Regoli calls that 2010 a "black year" for the Pope, specifically in relation to the tragic fatal accident that occurred to Manuela Camagni, one of the four Memores belonging to the small "Pontifical Family." I can certainly confirm this. In comparison with that misfortune, the media sensationalisms of those years - from the case of the traditionalist Bishop Williamson to a series of increasingly malicious attacks against the pope -, while having a certain effect, did not strike the pope's heart as much as Manuela's death, snatched so suddenly from our midst. Benedict was not an "actor pope," still less an insensitive "automaton pope"; even on the throne of Peter he was and remained a man; that is, as Conrad Ferdinand Meyer would say, he was not an "ingenious book," he was "a man with his own contradictions." That is how I myself got to know and appreciate him on a daily basis. And that is how it has remained until today.

Regoli observes, however, that after his last encyclical, *Caritas in Veritate* of Dec. 4, 2009, a dynamic, innovative pontificate with a strong charge from the liturgical, ecumenical and canonical points of view, it is as if he suddenly appeared "slowed down," blocked, bogged down. Although it is true that in later years the headwinds increased, I cannot confirm this judgment. His trips to the United Kingdom (2010), to Germany and Erfurt, Luther's city (2011), or to the fiery Middle East-from the concerned Christians of Lebanon (2012)-were all ecumenical milestones in these recent years. His decisive conduct in resolving the issue of abuse has been and remains a decisive indication of how to proceed. And when, before him, was there ever a pope who-along with his very serious task-also wrote books on Jesus of Nazareth that will perhaps also be regarded as his most important legacy?

It is not necessary here for me to dwell on how he, who was so affected by the sudden death of Manuela Camagni, later also suffered from the betrayal of Paul Gabriel, also a member of the same "Pontifical Family." And yet it is good for me to say once and for all with all clarity that Benedict ultimately did not resign because of the poor and misguided chamber aide, or because of the "delicacies" from his apartment that in the so-called "Vatileak affair" circulated in Rome as counterfeit currency but were traded in the rest of the world as authentic gold bars. No traitor or "crow" or any journalist could have pushed him to that decision. That scandal was too small for such a thing and all the greater the well-considered step of millennial historical significance that Benedict XVI took.

Regoli's exposition of these events also deserves consideration because he makes no claim to fully probe and explain this last, mysterious step; thus not further enriching that swarm of legends with further suppositions that have little or nothing to do with reality. And I too, an immediate witness to that spectacular and unexpected step by Benedict XVI, must admit that for it I am reminded again and again of the well-known and ingenious axiom with which in the Middle Ages John Duns Scotus justified the divine decree for the immaculate conception of the Mother of God:

"Decuit, potuit, fecit."

That is to say: it was a convenient thing, because it was reasonable. God could, therefore he did it. I apply the axiom to the decision of resignation in the following way: it was expedient, because Benedict XVI was aware that he was lacking the strength necessary for the very grave office. He could have done it, because he had long ago thought deeply, theologically, about the possibility of *popes emeriti* for the future. So he did.

The theologian pope's momentous resignation was a step forward essentially because on Feb. 11, 2013, speaking in Latin in front of surprised cardinals, he introduced the new institution of the "pope emeritus" in the Catholic Church, declaring that his strengths were no longer sufficient "to adequately exercise the Petrine ministry." The key word in that *Declaration* is *munus petrinum*, translated - as is most often the case - as "petrine ministry." And yet, *munus*, in Latin, has a multiplicity of meanings: it can mean service, task, guidance or gift, even prodigy. Before and after his resignation Benedict understood and understands his task as participation in such a "Petrine ministry." He left the papal throne and yet, with the step of February 11, 2013, he did not abandon this ministry at all. Instead, he has supplemented the personal office with a collegial and synodal dimension, almost a ministry in common, as if with this he wanted to reiterate once again the invitation contained in that motto that the then Joseph Ratzinger gave himself as Archbishop of Munich and Freising and which he then naturally kept as Bishop of Rome: "*cooperatores veritatis*," which means precisely "cooperators of the truth." In fact, it is not a singular but a plural, taken from the Third Epistle of John, in which it is written in verse 8: "We must welcome these people to become cooperators of the truth."

Since the election of his successor Francis on March 13, 2013, there are thus not two popes, but *de facto* an expanded ministry-with an active member and a contemplative member. This is why Benedict XVI did not give up either his name or the white cassock. That is why the correct appellation with which to address him even today is "Your Holiness"; and why, moreover, he did not retire to an isolated monastery, but within the Vatican - as if he had only stepped sideways to make room for his successor and for a new stage in the history of the papacy that he, with that step, enriched with the "central" of his prayer and compassion placed in the Vatican Gardens.

It was "the least expected step in contemporary Catholicism," Regoli writes, and yet a possibility on which Cardinal Ratzinger had reflected publicly as early as Aug. 10, 1978, in Munich in a homily on the occasion of Paul VI's death. Thirty-five years later he has not abandoned the office of Peter - something that would have been quite impossible for him following his irrevocable acceptance of the office in April 2005. Instead, by an act of extraordinary boldness he has renewed this office (even against the opinion of well-meaning and no doubt competent advisors) and with a final effort strengthened it (as I hope). This, of course, only history will be able to prove. But in the history of the Church it will remain that in the year 2013 the celebrated Theologian on the Threshold of Peter became the first "Pope Emeritus" in history. Since then his role - let me repeat it once again - is quite different from that of, for example, the saintly Pope Celestine V, who after his resignation in 1294 would have liked to return as a hermit, becoming instead a prisoner of his successor Boniface VIII (to whom we owe in the Church today the institution of the Jubilee years). Such a step as the one taken by Benedict XVI until today had precisely never been there. That is why it is not surprising that it has been perceived by some as revolutionary, or on the contrary, as absolutely in conformity with the Gospel; while still others see in this way the papacy secularized as never before, and with that more collegial and functional or even simply more human and less sacral. And still others are of the opinion that Benedict XVI, with this step, has almost - speaking in theological and historical-critical terms - demythologized the papacy.

In his overview of the pontificate, Regoli lays all this out clearly as never before. Perhaps the most moving part of the reading for me was the passage where, in a lengthy quotation, he recalls Benedict XVI's last general audience on February twenty-seven, 2013 when, under an unforgettable clear and terse sky, the Pope who would shortly thereafter resign summed up his pontificate this way:

It was a stretch of the Church's journey that had moments of joy and light, but also moments that were not easy; I felt like St. Peter with the Apostles in the boat on the Lake of Galilee: the Lord gave us many days of sunshine and light breezes, days when the fishing was abundant; there were also moments when the waters were rough and the wind contrary, as in the whole history of the Church, and the Lord seemed to be sleeping. But I have always known that in that boat is the Lord, and I have always known that the boat of the Church is not mine, it is not ours, but it is His. And the Lord does not let it sink; it is He who leads it, certainly also through the men He has chosen, because He has so willed. This has been and is a certainty, which nothing can tarnish.

I must admit that, rereading these words, almost tears could still come to my eyes, and all the more so for having seen firsthand and up close how unconditional, for himself and for his ministry, was Pope Benedict's adherence to the words of St. Benedict, whereby "nothing is to be put before the love of Christ," *nihil amori Christi praeponere*, as it is said in the rule handed down to us by Pope Gregory the Great. I witnessed it then, but I still remain fascinated by the precision of that last analysis in St. Peter's Square that sounded so poetic, but was nothing less than prophetic. In fact, they are words that today even Pope Francis immediately could and would undoubtedly subscribe to. Not to the popes but to Christ, to the Lord Himself, and to no one else belongs Peter's ship whipped by the waves of the stormy sea, when again and again we fear that the Lord is asleep and that He does not care about our needs, while all He needs is a single word to put an end to every storm; when instead it is our unbelief, our little faith and our impatience rather than the high waves and the howling of the wind that continually bring us down in panic.

Thus this book once again casts a consoling glance at the peaceful imperturbability and serenity of Benedict XVI, at the helm of Peter's boat during the dramatic years 2005-2013...

Archbishop Georg Gänswein, Prefect of the Papal Household
20 May 2016

"Dr. Mazza's timely and brilliant book provides the touchstone for interpreting the most tumultuous and bewildering events in Church history: the resignation of Benedict XVI and the subsequent election of Francis I. Mazza masterfully weaves historical and canonical insights to illuminate the explosive papal paradox-- the era of two popes. You will be spellbound by his penetrating analysis. At long last, Catholics will understand the enormity and significance of the Benedict resignation. Undoubtedly, this brave and stirring account will force a reckoning in the Catholic Church."

—**Liz Yore**, Esq.
Founder, YoreChildren.com

"Dr. Edmund Mazza is a true rarity in these days: a brilliant scholar who is willing to eschew his livelihood as a tenured establishment academic in service to the objective, observable truth...I am proud to call Dr. Ed my friend."

—**Ann Barnhardt**
Founder, *Barnhardt* Blog and Podcast

"There is much in Professors Mazza's book to recommend itself to the serious Catholic. If you want to take a deep dive into the history and meaning of the papacy...if you want to understand how Pope Benedict XVI resigned—yet didn't resign—his papal office, read this book."

—**Steve Mosher**
President, Population Research Institute

"Dr. Mazza's papacy book has the Gandalf 'enchantment' to break the spell of the sophistic professional Catholic 'Voices Saruman.' That Mazza 'enchantment' is truth, reason and groundbreaking research which will allow honest scholars to reject the false dichotomies of the Francis spin doctors."

—**Fred Martinez**
Founder, *The Catholic Monitor* Blog

Made in the USA
Las Vegas, NV
18 January 2024

84566725R00128